CHURCH USHERS
Embodiment of the Gospel

Kenneth M. Johnson

The Pilgrim Press
New York

Copyright © 1982 The Pilgrim Press
All rights reserved

No part of this publication may be reproduced, stored in a retrieval system, or transmitted in any form or by any means, electronic, mechanical, photocopying, recording, or otherwise (brief quotations used in magazines or newspaper reviews excepted), without the prior permission of the publisher.

Library of Congress Cataloging in Publication Data

Johnson, Kenneth M., 1928-
  Church ushers.

  1. Church ushers. I. Title.
  BV705.J63   254   81-21022
  ISBN 0-8298-0493-5 (pbk.)   AACR2

Biblical quotations in this book are from the *Revised Standard Version of the Bible,* copyright 1946, 1952 and © 1971 by the Division of Christian Education, National Council of Churches, and are used by permission.

The Pilgrim Press, 132 West 31 Street, New York, New York 10001

CONTENTS

	Introduction	5
1.	Called to Be Doorkeepers	7
	Doorkeepers in Ancient Times	7
	Doorkeepers in the Old Testament	9
	Doorkeepers in the New Testament	12
	Doorkeepers in Later Times	15
2.	Called to Be Ambassadors	20
	Ambassadors Who Stand for the Kingdom	20
	Ambassadors Who Represent the Body of Christ	23
	Ambassadors Who Love People	25
	Ambassadors Who Are Hospitable	28
3.	Called to Be Welcomers	33
	Welcomers with an Attractive Environment	33
	Welcomers with Effective Body Language	35
	Welcomers with Proper Closeness	40
4.	Called to Be Helpers	43
	Helpers Who Are Organized	43
	Helpers Who Are Trained	47
	Helpers Who Are Efficient	54
	Notes	60

INTRODUCTION

Church ushers are more than public relations officials; they are prominent dispensers of Christian love. Possibly my concept of ushers as embodiments of the gospel was born while I was a senior in high school. My family lived in the country, but occasionally I would go to the city to attend Sunday vespers. One night I visited a small Lutheran church. As I approached the door, a gentleman met me and extended his hand. "Welcome to our service," he began, and then introduced himself and asked my name. Then he introduced me to a man standing nearby. This expression of love toward me, a stranger, did much to enhance the worship experience.

After the service the two ushers spoke to me again—calling me by name and inviting me back. What a feeling of acceptance I experienced that night! The preacher, the sermon, the choir, and the congregation have been long forgotten. The church building has been torn down and a restaurant erected in its place. But the warmth expressed by these ushers lingers in my memory as if I had felt it last night. Jesus told his disciples, "Love one another as I have loved you [John 15:12]"; and the writer of 1 John concludes, "He who does not love his brother whom he has seen, cannot love God whom he has not seen [4:20]."

Another incident added to my interest in ushers. It happened during my first full-time pastorate, when Charles L. Allen was visiting preacher for a series of services at the large Methodist church downtown. At the time, Dr. Allen was preaching to overflow congregations at Grace Methodist Church, in Atlanta. (A few years later he became pastor of First United Methodist Church, in Houston, which became Methodism's largest congregation, with 12,000 members.) "Three things will fill a church sanctuary," he told a luncheon meeting in our church —"good music, helpful preaching, and effective ushers!" This comment stuck, so when the opportunity came for me to probe some aspect of church life in the Doctor of Ministry program at Drew University, I decided that ushers would be a worthy subject of study for this modern period. (I say "ushers" rather than "ushering" because the person and personal touch of the usher are far more significant than the mechanical function of ushering.) My experience in the project gave me the conviction that with study, training, and commitment, ushers can better appreciate the importance of their ministry; furthermore, church ushering can be elevated to an experience of sensitivity and care—fulfilling the biblical command to "practice hospitality [Rom. 12:13b]."

You will find in the following pages an eye-opening account of ushers both in their biblical and historical development. You will see how the usher's role has evolved from the gospel and discover how the relevant findings of psychology today relate to the subject. These chapters will stimulate people to attend and will enhance the effectiveness of pastoral care. Finally, you will be given "handles" for your local church—including a checklist of usher duties. A relevant prayer is included at the end of each chapter.

No longer does a church have to settle for ushering that is mediocre and uninspired. Ushers *are* an embodiment of the gospel in the local church. Their calling is never casual or routine. When they practice hospitality, ushers not only make a positive impression on visitors but they stimulate people to attend.

Kenneth M. Johnson

1
CALLED TO BE DOORKEEPERS

Ushers. The word suggests service to the church—greeting people and seating them, handing out bulletins, and collecting the offering. Ushers deal with practical matters. Those who work in this capacity do not usually regard themselves as set apart in calling or quality of life; however, their attire—along with flowers, badges, or other forms of identification—often does separate them from the rest of the congregation. They perform a useful and necessary function.

Doorkeepers in Ancient Times

Ostensibly, there is nothing new or novel about ushers. One may assume that, like the *King James Version* of the Bible, they have been around a long time, and rightly so. The word usher can be traced through Middle English *(ussher)*, Norman French *(usser)*, Old French *(ussier)*, Medieval Latin *(ustiarius)*, to the Latin *ostiarius*, meaning doorkeeper. While these terms do not refer exclusively to religious structures, they do describe church service. The relationship between ushers and ancient rites and customs, however, is not found in dictionaries. For the most part, traditional characteristics of ushering have been lost in the crosscurrents of history.

Rites of Passage

Ethnographer and folklorist Arnold van Gennep (1873-1957) is best remembered for the phrase rites de passage, to describe a person's activities in religious ceremonies, such as initiation rites, marriage, and funerals.[1] Such activities include the following elements: separation—especially prominent in funerals; transition—strongly emphasized in the marriage ceremony; and incorporation—such as the taking of membership vows. In this light we can see the usher's task as facilitating the rites of passage.

Sacred Space

In particular, a way of describing the usher's role is in terms of assisting people in moving from profane space (life in the world) to sacred space (life in the sanctuary).[2] The opening between the two is the threshold. "The threshold is the limit, the boundary, the frontier that distinguishes and opposes two worlds—and at the same time the paradoxical place where those worlds communicate, where passage from the profane to the sacred world becomes possible."[3] Based on this analysis, the usher may be considered an intermediary between two worlds, a kind of threshold escort.

The term sacred space has an interesting history. The presence of an altar is a distinguishing mark. In early Mesopotamia, for example, temple and house were indistinguishable except for the altar. The literal meaning of one Hebrew word for temple *(bayith)* is house.[4] In Isaiah 56:7 the temple is called a house of prayer *(beth tephillah)*.[5]

Body Movements

In ancient times the rites of passage commonly involved body movements denoting friendship and respect. Nonverbal means of communication—a bow, a prostration, a pious touch of the hand—were important parts of the entry ritual in home and temple.[6] Use of body language in today's ushering is, therefore, not without historical precedent.

Unfortunately, a gap between house and temple hospitality developed across the centuries. Today strangers tend to be treated better in the former than in the latter. A recent survey taken among ushers revealed the surprising opinion that it is important to greet people before a worship service but not afterward! One cannot imagine such treatment in the home—ancient or modern. The propriety of accompanying guests to the door is practiced in all civilized places. Appropriate gestures and words after a visit are a universal sign of good manners.

In fairness to doorkeepers it must be stated that their function historically centered on *entry* to places of worship; after the worshipers were inside ushers had no further responsibility.

Perhaps a difference in cordiality between house and temple developed as religion became institutionalized. Organization does tend to modify social interchange. Friendliness and informality in an intimate circle of people often give way to anonymity and indifference in a large organization. Maybe this is why someone recently signed the register in a colleague's church "A Complete Stranger."[7]

Doorkeepers in the Old Testament

The role of doorkeeper (*sho 'er* in Hebrew) has a long, colorful history. While the role may not be a model for ushers in the modern church, there is some connection. In 2 Kings 7:10 the function is broadened to include "gatekeepers of the city"; 2 Samuel 4:6 refers to a woman who was "doorkeeper of the house." Old Testament sources usually depict the doorkeeper as one who assisted worshipers into the temple, giving guidance and direction to those who could enter and those who could not. In Ezra 2:70 and 7:7 doorkeepers are listed with singers and temple servants. They were an integral part of temple worship.

Gatekeepers and Keepers of the Threshold

Gatekeeper is the dominant word in Nehemiah 7:1, 45, and 73, and in 1 Chronicles 15:18, 23-24, and 16:38. One assembly organized by David supposedly included four thousand gatekeepers (1 Chronicles 23:5); likewise, whole "divisions of the gatekeepers" are noted by the chronicler in 1 Chronicles 26:1, 12, and 19. In 2 Chronicles 8:14 reference is made to "gatekeepers in their divisions for the several gates." David "stationed the gatekeepers at the gates of the house of the Lord so that no one should enter who was in any way unclean [2 Chron. 23:19]." One verse in Chronicles states that "some of the Levites were scribes, and officials, and gatekeepers [2 Chron. 34:13]"— which means their task carried official status. Several Old Testament passages specifically refer to gatekeepers as keepers of the (temple) threshold: 2 Kings 12:9, 23:4, and 25:18; 2 Chronicles 34:9; Esther 2:21 and 6:2; and Jeremiah 35:4 and 52:24.

Herbert Huffmon, of Drew University, states that the Hebrew word *histpep,* which means literally to stand at the threshold, is misinterpreted in leading translations of Psalm 84:10b—the favorite proof-text of usher manuals. Instead of reading, "I would rather be a doorkeeper in the house of my God than dwell in the tents of wickedness"—indicating pleasure in the work—an amplified rendering of the text is, "If I have a choice between standing outside at the threshold (of the temple of Yahweh) or being inside the tent of the wicked one (some pagan deity), I choose to stand at the threshold."

The contemporary usher can relate to different elements of ushering in the Old Testament, but care must be taken in one's use of the different terms. "Doorkeepers," "gatekeepers," and "keepers of the threshold" sometimes overlap, even though the meaning of each term is distinct. "Gatekeeper" seems to have the broadest usage; the duties of the doorkeeper center on temple entry; the keeper of the threshold often exercises a more limited function, i.e., guarding the temple treasury.

Covenant

Other Old Testament images are more productive in shaping a model for the church usher. One example is the concept of covenant, an agreement between God and people, an agreement that included a brotherly regard for one's neighbor: "If your brother becomes poor, and cannot maintain himself with you, you shall maintain him; as a stranger and a sojourner he shall live with you [Lev. 25:35-36]." Another passage reads, "If there is among you a poor man, one of your brethren, in any of your towns within your land which the Lord your God gives you, you shall not harden your heart or shut your hand against your poor brother, but you shall open your hand to him [Deut. 15:7-8a]." Finally, the injunction "You shall love your neighbor as yourself [Lev. 19:18]"[8] is also quoted with hearty approval in the New Testament as part of the Great Commandment of Jesus. The ancient Jew felt God willed hospitality; therefore, negligence of any human need led to dire consequences for both the individual and the nation.

Porter

The *King James Version* uses the word porter for doorkeeper—a point of some confusion between British and American cultures. In the United States a porter is one who helps with luggage at a hotel or who waits on train passengers; in British usage, however, the porter is strictly a gatekeeper or doorman.[9]

Sojourners

Treatment of those who sojourned among the Hebrews deserves special attention, because there is a parallel between such persons and many people who attend church services today. In early Israel sojourners were not natives of the country in which they resided, nor were they regarded as foreigners; they were more like resident aliens. They were like many transient church members today—with one exception: Their status and position depended on the bond of hospitality that existed within particular families and/or communities. Old Testament examples are numerous: Abraham, a sojourner in Egypt (Genesis 12:10); Isaac, a sojourner with Abimelech, who protected him from maltreatment at the hands of the Philistines (Genesis 26:11); Jacob, a sojourner with Laban (Genesis 32:4); and Esau and Jacob, sojourners in the land of Canaan (Genesis 36:6-8).[10] "You shall not oppress a stranger," warns the writer of Exodus; "you know the heart of a stranger, for you were strangers in the land of Egypt [Exod. 23:9]." One Deuteronomist presents a similar view of sojourner: "For the Lord your God . . . is not partial and takes no bribe. He executes justice for the fatherless and the widow, and loves the sojourner, giving him food and clothing. Love the sojourner therefore; for you were sojourners in the land of Egypt [Deut. 10:17-19]."

Since all of us live on earth only temporarily, it could be said that all of us are sojourners. Mobility in contemporary church life makes the concept of sojourner more dramatic for some people than for others. A person who is transient and fails to form relationships is a case in point.

A survey taken about fifteen years ago in the Connecticut Conference of the United Church of Christ revealed that with each change in address people are less inclined to become involved. By their fourth move they become practically inactive in the church. Some inactivity may result from unwillingness to form friendships, only to have them broken after a short period. Rather than form ties that are short-lived, some persons decide to go it alone with their religious life.[11]

Hospitality

Although the Israelites formed a covenant community their concept of hospitality included other persons. Even before the Mosaic covenant, Genesis 12:1-3 puts it this way:

> Now the Lord said to Abram, "Go from your country and your kindred and your father's house to the land that I will show you. And I will make of you a great nation, and I will bless you, and make your name great, so that you will be a blessing. I will bless those who bless you, and him who curses you I will curse; and by you all the families of the earth will bless themselves."

This universal love for humankind was echoed by Deutero-Isaiah, who described God's covenant with the people as "a light to the nations [Isa. 42:6]." The prophet also wrote:

> Behold, you shall call nations that you know not,
>   and nations that knew you not shall run to you,
> because of the Lord your God, and of the Holy One of Israel,
>   for he has glorified you.
>   —Isaiah 55:5

A familiar passage from Trito-Isaiah reads:

> My house shall be called a house of prayer for all peoples.
> Thus says the Lord God,
>   who gathers the outcasts of Israel,
> I will gather yet others to him
>   besides those already gathered.
>   —Isaiah 56:7-8

Church signs that say "Everybody Welcome" have a measure of Old Testament backing.

How did a faithful Israelite honor Yahweh? According to early Israel, the deity was best honored in the concrete, not in the abstract. Performance of a task, a deed, or a function expressed gratitude to God. No higher motivation can be experienced by the church usher today.

Doorkeepers in the New Testament

Unlike the Old Testament, the New Testament does not take up the issue of entering (or leaving) the special meeting place. Even so, the word doorkeeper (*thuroros* in the Greek) does appear. The *Revised Standard Version* of the New Testament contains three doorkeeper passages:

> It is like a man going on a journey, when he leaves home and puts his servants in charge, each with his work, and commands the *doorkeeper* to be on the watch.
>   —Mark 13:34

> To him the *gatekeeper* opens; the sheep hear his voice, and he calls his own sheep by name and leads them out.
>   —John 10:3

> Simon Peter followed Jesus, and so did another disciple. As this disciple was known to the high priest, he entered the court of the high priest along with Jesus, while Peter stood outside at the *door.* So the other disciple, who was known to the high priest, went out and spoke to the maid who *kept the door,* and brought Peter in. The maid who *kept the door* said to Peter, "Are not you also one of this man's disciples?" He said, "I am not."
>   —John 18:15-17

Hospitality

Despite the limited occurrence of "doorkeeper" in the New Testament, the concept of Christian hospitality is quite prominent. Hospitality was and remains an important element in Christianity. In a writing that preceded the Gospels, Paul urged, "Contribute to the needs of the saints, practice *hospitality* [Rom. 12:13]." Some years later the Epistle to the Hebrews, thinking of Genesis, counseled, "Do not neglect to show *hospitality* to strangers, for thereby some have entertained angels unawares [Heb. 13:2]." Granted a more advanced reflection on duties of church officials in the pastoral epistles, the continued emphasis on hospitality is clear. For instance, the responsible widow must not only raise her children properly, she is also urged to be hospitable: "She must be well attested for her good deeds, as one who has brought up children, shown *hospitality,* washed the feet of the saints, relieved the afflicted, and devoted herself to doing good in every way [1 Tim. 5:10]."

In the beginning it was people—not documents—that spread the good news about Jesus.[12] It was the spoken word and the human voice that carried the message of God's love. Paul and his companions, the most prominent propagators of the Christian faith, traveled by foot and by boat to deliver their message. Unlike their modern counterparts, migrating Christians could expect to be entertained by fellow Christians where they stopped en route. The *Didache,* an early document that described church regulations, stated the matter in quaint and humorous terms—to us, not to them:

> Let everyone that "cometh in the name of the Lord" be received: then, when ye have proved him, ye shall know, for ye can know the right hand from the left. If he that cometh be a passer-by, give him all the help ye can; but he shall not stay, except, if there be need, two or three days. If he wish to abide with you, being a craftsman, let him work and eat. If he have no craft, use your common sense to provide that he may live with you as a Christian, without idleness. If he be unwilling so to do, he is a "Christ-monger." Beware of such (XII).[13]

Hospitality was widespread in the early church: Peter was entertained by Simon the Tanner and by Mary (John Mark's mother); Paul was entertained by Lydia, in Philippi; in Corinth, Paul enjoyed the hospitality of Prisca and Aquila, who also received Apollos; and when Apollos went from Ephesus to Corinth, Prisca and Aquila provided him with a letter urging that he be received there.[14]

House Churches

House churches were common in New Testament times. Paul's letters refer to and assume hospitality in this area of church life. Philemon and the individuals cited in Romans 16 are examples. House churches are implied in the Gospels, when Jesus instructed the disciples to take no money or baggage with them on their journey (cf. Mark 6:7-11; Matthew 10:5-42; and Luke 9:2-5; 10:1-16). He assumed hospitality would be provided by the people to whom the disciples were sent.

Foot-washing

Was the foot-washing described in John 13:3-10 an act of hospitality? Perhaps. The custom of a host or hostess washing his or her guest's feet was part of early Christian tradition. The practice continues today in some churches. Hospitality undoubtedly played an important role in the rise and spread of the Christian movement.

The Church at Dura: A Model of Hospitality

A possible picture of early Christian hospitality is suggested by one of the archaeological digs at Dura, on the Euphrates in eastern Syria.[15] As one walks down Wall Street in Dura the remains of three religious shrines may be viewed: Mithraeum, where the Persian god Mithra was worshiped; a synagogue that was converted from a private house; and an unimposing building used by the newer sect, the Christians. Like the synagogue, the Christian shrine was made over from a private house and had only one room.

> The walls of the room are covered with badly faded, rather crude paintings—these Christians obviously could not afford an artist of the quality used by the Mithraists and the Jews.
> Above the basin is the familiar figure of "the good shepherd" . . . just beneath him, a small drawing of a naked couple taking fruit from a tree, observed by a snake. On the north wall, to the right of the basin, a procession of women approach a tomb, the pediment of which is adorned by two imposing stars.
> Just above, there is a scene showing a man lying on a bed and, again, carrying the bed, while a man in white chiton and himation makes a gesture usually associated with magic or miracle. A fragmentary scene shows men in a boat, with two figures apparently standing on the water.[16]

The Dura model of Christianity attests to the fact that our ancestors in the faith were poor compared to the local Jews and the Mithraists—but they were not penniless. We may also assume the function of the usher, if not the office, in early Christianity. What made our forebears unique was the impact Jesus and the resurrected Christ had on their lives. This living faith catapulted them across the world in a loving ministry characterized by a strong element of hospitality—hospitality not just to their own kind but to needy people everywhere.

Doorkeepers in Later Times

According to Pope Cornelius, Roman church officials in A.D. 250 consisted of 46 presbyters, 7 regional deacons, 7 subdeacons, 42 acolytes, 52 exorcists, lectors, *doorkeepers,* and about 1,500 widows.[17] While threading through the labyrinth of early church history, I found that "doorkeeper" is translated in the Latin as *ostiarius* and as *janitor;* kindred English words that followed are porter, sacristan, custodian, and verger. The duties of each take on changes peculiar to the different periods of church history but remain identifiable with their predecessor offices.

Patristic Period

Between the third and seventh centuries preliminary steps toward ordination into the priesthood included the Minor Order of Ostiarius, or Doorkeeper. Such steps were meaningful preparatory rites, taking place at the altar yet separate from the eucharistic service. Initiation into a minor order was structured into a formal service of recognition, with responsibilities that were spelled out. For example, the doorkeeper's duties were as follows: "To the doorkeeper it appertains to ring the bell, to open the church doors and the sacristy, and to open the book of the preacher."[18] The doorkeeper was also given keys as the insignia of the office. The job began to take on more of a functional pattern than in earlier times.

By the end of the fourth century the Order of Doorkeeper had become a less prominent step toward the priesthood. It no longer figured in the letters of popes, and apparently, its members became servants of a lower grade when their general education was insufficient for service in higher offices. At the Council of Trullo, in 692, Justinian II expressed the belief that the doorkeeper was no longer a constituent part of the hierarchy.[19]

While the minor orders in the East eventually merged into subdiaconates, they continued in the West until they were made installations by Pope Paul VI, in 1972.[20] Until recently, the tradition of doorkeeper has been kept as a step for seminarians; however, functions of the order were assumed by the laity centuries ago.[21]

One could fantasize about the role of ushers during the patristic and early medieval periods—seeing it as a positive, affirming, and supportive role—but actually, doorkeepers also kept unbelievers and notorious sinners out of the sanctuary. While this development seems harsh against the backdrop of New Testament hospitality, it must be seen as the church fathers' effort to keep the faith pure. Fr. Robert B.

Eno, of the Department of Theology at The Catholic University of America, Washington, DC, cautions those who would describe Christian hospitality during the patristic period:

> In general, I would warn against confusing general Christian hospitality such as taking strangers (normally other Christians) into one's home, feeding them, etc., with specific Eucharistic hospitality which would normally be much more restrictive (open to those who are baptized, orthodox in belief and lead a moral life—Justin Martyr).[22]

Medieval and Reformation Periods

After the patristic period the church became a more closely knit social structure. During the medieval period, hospitality centered in the monasteries. These were the community centers of the Middle Ages; they served as combined departments of social services, hospitals, and places for spiritual guidance. The role of doorkeeper is virtually missing from literature for a long stretch of church history—from medieval times, through the Reformation, until the nineteenth century. Despite my reluctance to assign twelve centuries to a simple sentence, the absence of any primary source material on ushering for this period forces me to do just that!

Modern Period: Dwight L. Moody

Church ushering in the United States became visible in the work of shoe-salesman-turned-evangelist Dwight L. Moody (1837-99). Large audiences at the Moody-Sankey revivals necessitated some type of crowd control. Moody, who daily crammed 11,000 people into his New York meetings over a four-month period in early 1876, saw ushering as an answer to crowd management. Wiser in the ways of the business world than his fellow preachers, he saw the value of ushers. A smashing evangelistic success on both sides of the Atlantic, Moody was particular about his ushers and personally hired 500 men to seat the crowds at the New York revival.[23] Church historian Bernard A. Weisberger cites an example from the year before, in 1875, in the big Philadelphia campaign: "Ushers were chosen and trained, along with a new breed of Christian helpers called 'inquiry room workers.'"[24]

Phineas Bresee and Ambrose Clark

Two contrasting examples of usher emerged in the 1890s: Phineas F. Bresee, founder of the Nazarene Church, and Ambrose R. Clark, organizer of the first board of ushers in New York City. Ushering practices initiated by Bresee in his Los Angeles church are documented by historian Timothy L. Smith:

> Before each service, Bresee would stand at the door and welcome every worshiper. If a man came in poor clothing and with obvious embarrassment, the pastor would put his arm around him and usher him to the best seat in the house. Whenever he greeted anyone, at whatever time of day, Bresee said, "Good morning." It was always morning for the Christian, he said, for their eyes were fixed on heaven.[25]

On the East Coast, Clark was instructing his ushers in a different philosophy: "Ushering is the art of making the church member and visitor feel comfortably at home and of lending spiritual dignity to the whole church service."[26] Conversations about a church ushers' organization were held by Clark in March 1910, and on January 19, 1914, the Church Ushers Association of New York was formally established. In the beginning most of the churches belonging to the association were located on Fifth Avenue, and included Fifth Avenue Baptist, Marble Collegiate, Fifth Avenue Presbyterian; soon other prominent churches became involved—Broadway Tabernacle, Madison Avenue Methodist Episcopal, Madison Square Presbyterian, and the Cathedral Church of Saint John the Divine.

Initially, twenty-three churches were represented in the Church Ushers Association of New York. In addition to local church activity, this organization provided ushering for Billy Sunday's New York campaign in 1916, the Temple of Religion services at the New York World's Fair in 1939 and 1940, and the annual Easter Dawn services at Radio City Music Hall.[27]

National United Church Ushers Association

While the progressive leadership of Ambrose R. Clark put New York in the vanguard of church ushering, few references to the work are found in late nineteenth- and early twentieth-century literature. For example, ushering is conspicuous by its absence from the standard work of Washington Gladden, *Church and Parish Problems* (subtitled *Vital Hints and Helps for Pastors, Officers, and People)*, published in 1911.[28] Even though published comments are rare, ushering became a regular practice in churches, especially those in urban centers. This is evidenced by the organization of the National United Church Ushers Association, in 1919. Annual national conventions of this association, with representatives from predominantly black congregations, now attract 2,500 to 3,000 delegates from numerous local chapters in twenty-one states. The membership numbers around 100,000 and includes more women than men.[29]

Garrett Manual

The earliest book on church ushering that I discovered is *Church Ushers' Manual,* written by Willis O. Garrett and published in 1924. Author Garrett used an interesting subtitle: *A Handbook for Church Ushers and All Others Who Would Promote the Spirit of Fellowship in the House of God.*[30] Garrett established the historical connections between modern ushering and the biblical faith but did not fill in the gaps.

Andy Frain's Ushers Union

Ushering took a giant step forward in a movement that started in 1927. This year is normally remembered as the year in which Charles A. Lindbergh made his historic first solo nonstop flight from New York to Paris, but it was also a year in which something important to ushers happened in Chicago. While this Chicago event did not occur in a church, it was destined to influence church ushering greatly. Andy Frain, a former soda pop and cushion salesman at Comiskey Park and Wrigley Field, initiated his own ushering system to counter the disorder and confusion the patrons experienced when they attended baseball games. Frain started out with badges for the ushers; later, caps, sweaters, and trousers were purchased. When the fledging group of ushers came to the attention of William Wrigley Jr., 350 blue and gold uniforms were ordered.

Andy Frain's Ushers' Union soon spread nationwide, providing professionally trained ushers for sports, political, social, and even church events. In 1939 the man who had switched from cushions to seating was presented the Catholic Youth Organization Club of Champions medal. In making the presentation, Auxiliary Bishop Bernard J. Sheil of Chicago said, "This award has been given to you for outstanding service in helping the youth of America. You have helped more young men through high schools and colleges than any other individual in America."[31]

In 1964, Andy Frain died of a heart attack in Rochester, Minnesota, at age fifty-nine. His body was taken to his beloved Chicago for burial. A requiem mass was celebrated at Queen of All Saints Roman Catholic Church, with Bishop Cletus O'Donnell of Chicago, a former Frain usher, officiating. In *The New York Times* obituary it was estimated that more than 25,000 youth—men and women—had worn Frain uniforms, including thousands who had worked their way through college.[32] Since 1932 the Frain organization had handled nine national political conventions. Andy's last big assignments were in early 1964: the Sonny Liston-Cassius Clay heavyweight title fight and a dinner for President Lyndon B. Johnson, both in Miami. "Andrew Thomas Frain preferred to be called a crowd engineer, but he was known as the 'king of the ushers.' His ticket-takers, plainclothesmen and seat-escorters supervised the conduct of an estimated 50 million persons each year."[33]

Other Contributors

Other persons also made important contributions to ushering. E.H. Hosman, head of the extension program at the University of Omaha, originated a course on church ushering in the early 1940s; his first class graduated in 1944. Dr. Hosman also offered the course in other parts of the country and by correspondence.[34] In 1957 Mark R. Moore published his manual, *The Ministry of Ushering*.[35] Dr. Moore made an important contribution with his title and his historical references, which fill in some of the gaps of church ushering since the turn of the century.

Publications that give attention to the mechanics of church ushering include *A Guide to Church Ushering*, by Homer J.R. Elford (1961); *The Work of the Usher*, by Alvin D. Johnson (1966); *The Usher's Manual*, by Leslie Parrott (1970); and *Church Usher: Servant of God*, by David R. Enlow (1980).[36]

It seems ironic that a service as visible and important as ushering should be so lightly regarded by historians and theologians. Tacticians have generally done a good job of reviving the mechanics of the art but have accomplished little more. Meanwhile, it is my thesis that attention to our roots reveals significant historical and theological insights that elevate ushering to a real experience of hospitality, i.e, as a form of incarnational service.

An Usher's Prayer

God, my job as doorkeeper is no small assignment. I recognize the significance of this ministry, helping people from the world to worship and then from the experience of worship to go back into the world refreshed and renewed.

In serving as doorkeeper, I do something tangible and visible in expressing my love for you and your love for others. Mine is an acted parable; therefore, help me to be hospitable in the performance of my duties, treating others as I would like to be treated.

Enable me to be helpful, conveying to all a sense of your welcome and presence. Through Jesus Christ, the Master Doorkeeper. Amen.

2
CALLED TO BE AMBASSADORS

Early in 1981, millions throughout the world watched their television sets as a momentous event unfolded. When the fifty-two American hostages freed from Iran stepped off the Air Algerie plane in Algiers, we witnessed the first dramatic installment in their return to freedom. Our eyes were glued to our sets as we saw these bedraggled yet elated returnees being greeted by the chief American negotiator, U.S. Deputy Secretary of State Warren Christopher. Nearest to the camera in the receiving line at the Algiers airport was a tall, soft-spoken gentleman who said to the returning Americans, "I am Ulrich Haynes, Ambassador to Algeria. Welcome!"

What is an ambassador?

Americans will answer that an ambassador is an official representative of the United States in a foreign land who not only speaks for the United States, but who also holds the honor of the country in his or her hands. Paul and other apostolic leaders of the early church also claimed to be ambassadors, i.e., representatives of a sovereign ruler. They claimed to act for and on behalf of Christ. "We are ambassadors for Christ, God making his appeal through us [2 Cor. 5:20]."

All Christians are ambassadors by virtue of their baptism. They are citizens of two worlds: the earthly nation into which they are born and the kingdom of God, into which they are reborn. For the church usher, who is responsible for assisting people in their passage between the two worlds, the title of ambassador seems especially appropriate.

Ambassadors Who Stand for the Kingdom

What about the ambassadorial role of a church usher? The identity of a church usher is theological in nature, which is to say it comes from God. The duties of an usher, therefore, include standing for God's rule and reign—the kingdom, representing the Body of Christ, loving people, and dispensing hospitality.

The Usher's Authority

In some churches the usher is identified by dress, coat and slacks, badge, or flower. However, such symbols fail to communicate the true source of authority. The analogy of an American ambassador, who serves at the pleasure of the President, may help us better understand the authorization for the work. It may be said that the church usher serves at the pleasure of God—not just at the request of a head usher or a pastor. David Enlow, an active layman, emphasized this idea by titling his recently published manual *Church Usher: Servant of God*.[1]

Another way of describing the kingdom representation of ushering is to compare it with other forms of ushering. In the theater, for example, an usher is hired by the management to seat patrons and has a responsibility to the manager for the performance of duties. Ushering in the religious establishment is not as clear-cut on the "organizational charts"—especially when throngs crowd a doorway or when all the pews have been taken. Accountability to some person in charge may be necessary, but beyond this organizational necessity the church usher is on his or her own and must use persuasion, not force, to assist people. The church usher is not simply a crowd engineer; rather, this servant is a unique communicator of God's rule and is expected to be accepting, compassionate, and patient. To become such an usher is to adopt a kingdom life-style in one's attitudes and actions. In this way a church usher is both a servant of God and of people.

Loss of this kingdom identity may account for some of the recent shift in emphasis from people to function. As one respondent to a recent usher questionnaire put it, "I make a distinction between ushering and greeting." The time has come for the church to reassert its kingdom authority for ushers, snatching them from the clutches of secular models and shifting the focus of their work from system back to ministry and from function back to service.

The kingdom, or rule of God, has never been fully accepted, not even by the Israelites.[2] Because of this reluctance, there arose within the Hebrew tradition a hope for such a reign in the future. The Hebrews believed the consummation of kingdom rule would take place after the "day of the Lord"—a time when God would triumphantly intervene to establish the kingdom finally and completely. Against this mind-set of the kingdom, John the Baptist appeared, preaching, "Repent, for the kingdom of heaven is at hand [Matt. 3:2]."

The idea of kingdom occupied a central place in the teachings of Jesus. He used the phrase to refer to God's rule in the present order and in future time. Thus, when we pray the Lord's Prayer, we petition "thy kingdom come [Matt. 6:10 and Luke 11:2]." The imminence or nowness of the kingdom is implied by what Jesus said about his miracles (see Luke 7:22 and Matthew 11:4-5). A present reality of the kingdom of God is explicit in Luke 17:20-21: "Being asked by the Pharisees when the kingdom of God was coming, he answered them, 'The kingdom of God is not coming with signs to be observed; nor will they say, "Lo, here it is!" or "There!" for behold, the kingdom of God is in the midst of you.'"

Despite the biblical importance of "kingdom" the usher may still not see its connection with such work. What is the relationship between the kingdom of God and church ushering? Since God's reign is characterized by helping people, the usher's work may be seen as a manifestation of the kingdom, as in Mark 4:26-29:

> And he said, "The kingdom of God is as if a man should scatter seed upon the ground, and should sleep and rise night and day, and the seed should sprout and grow, he knows not how. The earth produces of itself, first the blade, then the ear, then the full grain in the ear. But when the grain is ripe, at once he puts in the sickle, because the harvest has come."

Even though the church usher—along with other disciples—awaits completion of the kingdom, she or he is privileged to participate in kingdom-building. Such activity never takes place in a vacuum; invariably a social dimension is involved. Furthermore, Jesus insisted that service to the kingdom takes precedence over other duties. For example, when one of the disciples expressed his wish to attend his father's funeral, Jesus stressed kingdom priorities by answering, "Leave the dead to bury their own dead; but as for you, go and proclaim the kingdom of God [Luke 9:60]." In another place, one reads the challenging words, "No one who puts his hand to the plow and looks back is fit for the kingdom of God [Luke 9:62]." Single-minded attention and devotion—these were Jesus' requirements for those engaged in kingdom work. The call to ushering involves more than agreement to serve in a particular time frame; faithfulness with one's agreement to serve is what counts. "Not every one who says to me, 'Lord, Lord,' shall enter the kingdom of heaven, but he who does the will of my Father who is in heaven [Matt. 7:21]."[3]

Those ambassadors who meet us at church events, who greet us and help us with the service, are sensitive to people needs. At the same time, however, they are responsible to God, at whose pleasure they serve. This theological dimension to the usher's work is recognized by Matthew when he writes of the coveted response of every usher: "Well done, good and faithful servant; you have been faithful over a little, I will set you over much; enter into the joy of your master [Matt. 25:21]."

Ambassadors Who Represent the Body of Christ

While authority for the usher's task is derived from the kingdom of God, this authority also relates to the local congregation. The usher is an ambassador of goodwill who represents the Body of Christ, the church.

What is a local church? In his definitive work on images of the church, Paul S. Minear cited ninety-six different New Testament images or analogies.[4] Among the more prominent ones is the Body of Christ. "Just as the body is one and has many members, and all the members of the body, though many, are one body, so it is with Christ. . . . Now you are the body of Christ and individually members of it [1 Cor. 12:12, 27]." In using the image of body, Paul emphasized the interdependence that exists between members of a local congregation, a relationship requiring a mutual kinship with Christ. The usher, then, does more than connect people with people; indeed, he or she represents the Head as well as the members of the Body in the performance of certain duties. The usher's time and talent are directed primarily toward building, affirming, and supporting the work of the Body. In short, the usher's ministry is a ministry of love. "The image of the body and the image of love should for all significant purposes be considered one image; they cannot, in fact, be considered otherwise, since the primary content of both is determined by the image of Christ."[5]

Embodiment of the Gospel

Danish philosopher and theologian, Sören Kierkegaard affirmed that "in order to be Christians, we have to become contemporaneous with Christ."[6] Therefore, the work of the usher may rightly be considered the extension or embodiment of the incarnation.

When "the Word became flesh and dwelt among us [John 1:14]," God acted in a community of people to incarnate God's will and way. One of the first things Jesus did was to build community by recruiting twelve men "to be with him [Mark 3:14]." The twelve initial disciples became the foundation stones of the New Community, the *ecclesia* (church). A hymn by John Mason Neale captures the essence of this act:

> His twelve apostles first he made
>   His ministers of grace;
> And they their hands on others laid,
>   To fill in turn their place.
>
> So age by age, and year by year,
>   His grace was handed on;
> And still the holy church is here,
>   Although her Lord is gone.[7]

Thus, the church is the extension of the incarnation, and its ushers embody this incarnation at the threshold. Embodiment brings life and breath and vitality and personality into an otherwise routine duty. Embodiment is more than the power of positive thinking; it is the reception of God's grace and the communication of this grace through a human instrument called an usher.

Once ushering in the church takes on the vision of embodiment of the gospel, it can never be viewed as mechanical service. It is, in fact, part of a divine drama, with God the principal actor and the usher identifying with and responding to cues in an unfolding scene of revelation. Just as no two performances of a play can ever be alike, so no two experiences of ushering can be the same. Each ushering experience is new, fresh, and varied. Because the usher is a representative of the local church —the first to meet and, theoretically, the last to greet—his or her role of embodiment is critical to the communication of the gospel. When applied to an usher, the gospel means "God's glad acceptance of people."

Church

Earliest descriptions of the church in the New Testament come from the apostle Paul, whose letters predate the Gospels by several years. Robin Scroggs summarized the character of the early church as a community in which the joyous feelings of liberation were shared; the reciprocal pronoun is prominent.[8] "Love one another with brotherly affection; outdo one another in showing honor [Rom. 12:10]." "Live in harmony with one another [Rom. 12:16]." "Welcome one another, therefore, as Christ has welcomed you [Rom. 15:7]." The implications for ushers are self-evident.

Another characteristic of the early church was its disregard of societal or economic status. As has often been said, "Everyone stands on level ground at the cross." People have different talents and capacities—some are weak, some are strong. But before God all are equal. While distinctions between persons are inevitable—and even necessary—value judgments are not to be made.[9]

Women as Ushers

The black church in America has a long, noble tradition of using women as ushers. Other progressive churches are discovering that women possess unique gifts of sensitivity and care at different levels of leadership, including ushering. Rachel Conrad Wahlberg rightly asserts: "The church can only benefit if full ability, insight and performance are expected from 100% of its members, not just the male 45%. The goal of Christians is to be neither Greek nor Jew, neither slave nor free, neither male nor female, but full persons doing the work of Jesus Christ."[10]

Can it be that women are not mentioned as ushers in manuals published to date because all the authors of such manuals are males? Or can it be that women are not mentioned because, until recently, they were not asked to serve as ushers?[11]

Ambassadors Who Love People

The love attitude was exemplified by Jesus. Those who try to follow his lead understand the concept better than the practice. Jesus had an uncanny way of loving people, as though there were only one of them to love. He loved people as they were, not as he wanted them to be or as he wanted them to become. Recall the understanding words he spoke concerning the woman taken in adultery—"Let him who is without sin among you be the first to throw a stone after her [John 8:7]"—and to Zacchaeus, a despised tax collector, who was perched in a sycamore tree—"Zacchaeus, make haste and come down; for I must stay at your house today [Luke 19:5]." In his great hymn of love Paul concluded, "So faith, hope, love abide, these three; but the greatest of these is love [1 Cor. 13:13]."

Indifference

Monotony of the work is detrimental in ushering, epecially when the usher becomes preoccupied with the system. All aspects of worship risk becoming automatic and routine—standing, kneeling, affirming, singing, and even praying. Therefore, the alert usher is on guard against indifference. Love can easily be short-circuited when the usher allows his or her mind to wander or when he or she becomes mechanical and insensitive. An anonymous author has addressed the concern this way: "God does not will to draw any love exclusively to himself; He wills that we should love Him 'in our neighbor.' The true opposite of love is not hate but indifference. Hate, bad as it is, at least treats the neighbor as a person; whereas, indifference turns the neighbor into an it, a thing."[12] Norman A. Derosiers, who wears the hat of a United Methodist clergyman and of a psychiatrist, perceived that "nothing, absolutely nothing, will more consistently drive persons out of the church than indifference to their presence. Feelings that their presence does not mean anything to anyone or that no one really cares to know anything about them or to establish a relationship with them is cause enough to lead them elsewhere."[13]

For many people, love is not only many-splendored, but also fuzzy. One reason for this is the term in English Bibles is all-encompassing, whereas in the original Greek of the New Testament, different words for love appear. *Eros* (sexual love), *philia* (the affection between friends), *storge* (family love), and *agape* (God's love) are the most prominent examples. The Gospels are especially replete with instances of agape, such as in Luke 15, where one reads about a lost sheep, a lost coin, and a lost son.

More important than Jesus' words about love were his deeds that demonstrated love: "The Son of man has come eating and drinking; and you say, 'Behold, a glutton and a drunkard, a friend of tax collectors and sinners!' [Luke 7:34]." Jesus embodied love, but it took his disciples until Pentecost for the full measure of Christ's love to sink in. After Pentecost, however, the followers of Jesus were able to claim, "God was in Christ reconciling the world to himself [2 Cor. 5:19]." Part of the church usher's opportunity is to embody Christ's love to others. The good news of the gospel is that we are loved (see John 3:16); the good news for the church usher, the ambassador of goodwill, is that God's love is expressed through the usher to others. Ushering incorporates God's love in a function that otherwise appears to be a menial task, a routine activity, or simply busywork. The biblical vision presents a different picture. Here the Holy Spirit assists the usher to become an embodiment of love; to the extent that this happens, the kingdom of God is realized.

Satisfactions

What are the satisfactions of ushering? An unknown author has answered the question this way:

> There are glorious chapters in the history of Christian love. Mary, visited by the Most High, cherished in her heart a divinely unselfish love for her son Jesus.
>
> As Jesus grew in wisdom, stature, and in favor with God and man, he went about His Father's business of love.
>
> The twelve disciples answered His call to forsake all to follow Him and to learn together how to live in this love.
>
> Other disciples after Pentecost formed a beloved community, shared all their things in common, rejoiced and served God. In the face of persecution many Christians were faithful unto death, like torches in a dark world bearing witness to a new light of love. Convinced believers in this way of love lay aside property and position to become little brothers of the poor, going forth to minister to any in need.
>
> Missionaries gave up home and security to live in foreign lands as messengers of the gospel of love.

Reforming spirits called Protestants were determined to correct the evil abuses of their day and to create new communities where love and democracy could unite in freedom to worship God.

Churches and schools arose on the frontiers, social settlements arose in the slums, to bring new birth in spiritual love.

Fellowships of suffering and service have raised funds and brought vital goods to starving and homeless enemies in the reconciling forgiveness of love.[14]

I hope our churches will soon be able to add the following to this statement of love: "Church ushers, Christ's doorkeepers and ambassadors, have in recent years caught the vision of an embodied gospel—reaching out in love and affection to strangers and friends alike, creating an atmosphere of freedom and acceptance in the gathered community."

While our family was traveling in another state one summer we spotted a United Methodist church to the right. I turned the car around and parked it. This dreamy, little southern town was most attractive at 10:45 on Sunday morning. As we walked from our car toward the church we were impressed by the neat lawns and colorful flowers. When we reached the doors leading into the sanctuary, we found, to our surprise, that they were locked! We could not understand this, because it was almost time for the service to begin and people were milling about on the grounds and in other sections of the building. We walked down the steps and, following the lead of others, through a side door. No usher was seen or heard.

As I entered the sanctuary, I saw a small stack of bulletins lying on a radiator cover. Each of us picked up one, and we found our own way to a pew. Other people straggled in and nodded and spoke to each other—but not to us! Soon the organist began to play the prelude, and the choir and minister entered through a chancel door and processed. I tried not to let our cool reception bother me too much, because I am aware that not all ushers recognize the need to welcome the visitor. My family and I felt some kinship with the minister when he mentioned that this was only the second Sunday he had served this church. "I am still trying to find my way about," he confessed. So were we! I do remember one redemptive act in this experience, however. After the benediction a kindly old woman seated nearby greeted us and told us she was glad we had attended the service. Her love communicated itself beautifully to us. For the usher, however, it was a missed opportunity for satisfactions that come to the thoughtful doorkeeper.

Ambassadors Who Are Hospitable

One who welcomes guests with warmth and generosity is said to be hospitable. The word is especially applicable to one who is well disposed toward strangers. To have an open and charitable mind toward people like oneself is easy; the rub comes when one confronts those who are not. The tendency is to be suspicious of those whose dress and deportment are different.

As mentioned earlier, hospitality is not uniquely Jewish or Christian; it goes back to primitive cultures, where it was a method of survival. In ancient times today's host could be tomorrow's traveler. There were no Holiday Inns. The more people one could accommodate under one's roof, the greater the protection against intruders and/or robbers. To be hospitable in primitive societies, therefore, was a deeply ingrained custom.

Christian Hospitality

In the Christian era, hospitality continued from the past—but with a different motive. No longer was hospitality viewed as a matter of self-interest; rather, it was transformed into deeds of unselfish service, and was offered in the spirit and manner of Jesus Christ, without any thought of recompense or reward.

The wise writings of Henri J.M. Nouwen probe the subject of hospitality in the contemporary setting, expressing the belief that the world is full of strangers—people estranged from their pasts, cultures, and countries; from their neighbors, friends, and families; from their deepest selves and their God. According to Nouwen, people are desperately seeking hospitable places where life can be lived without fear and where community can be found.

> Although many, we might even say most, strangers in this world become easily the victim of a fearful hostility, it is possible for men and women and obligatory for Christians to offer open and hospitable space where strangers can cast off their strangeness and become our fellow human beings.[15]

Despite risks, Nouwen argues, our Christian vocation is to convert the *hostis* (hostility) into a *hospes* (hospitality), the enemy into a guest, and to create the free and fearless space where brotherhood and sisterhood can be experienced.

Instructional sheets on church ushering invariably point to one's smile as an important part of the job description. Of course, I am not against smiling, but there is a danger in such exhortations, i.e., the perpetuation of what Nouwen calls "soft sweet kindness, tea parties, bland conversations and a general atmosphere of coziness." Such is not the essence of New Testament hospitality. If genuine caring lies behind the smile, then well and good; if, however, the smile is plastic and insincere, the stranger is apt to pick up on the artificial and be unimpressed. Nouwen suggests a meaningful model when he describes hospitality as "the creation of a free space, where the stranger can enter and become a friend."[16]

Listening

Another approach to hospitality is presented in the play *Shear Madness,* which played to sold-out houses for more than a year in Boston. In this mystery-comedy a murder is committed, and all characters become suspect. Part of the genius of this production lay in the involvement of the audience in questioning the cast about the murder. The producer instructed the cast to listen carefully to the comments and questions. If the audience were not *heard,* the play would be less effective.

Christian hospitality involves listening. Words spoken in the narthex can be meaningless chatter that is neither received nor responded to appropriately. An interesting exercise for an usher might be to sit down after a service and prepare a verbatim write-up of her or his conversations before and after a service. Chances are the exercise would produce better listeners on the usher board.

Being alert to worshipers' needs, and responding politely and with interest to the spoken word and to nonverbal signals are sure ways of becoming an effective ambassador. Nobody has said it better than Dietrich Bonhoeffer:

> The first service that one owes to others in the fellowship consists of listening to them. Just as love to God begins with listening to His Word, so the beginning of love for the brethren is learning to listen to them. It is God's love for us that He not only gives us His Word but also lends us His ear. . . .
>
> Many people are looking for an ear that will listen. They do not find it among Christians, because these Christians are talking where they should be listening. But he who can no longer listen to his brother will soon be no longer listening to God either; he will be doing nothing but prattle in the presence of God, too. . . .
>
> One who cannot listen long and patiently will presently be talking beside the point and be never really speaking to others albeit he be not conscious of it. Anyone who thinks that his time is

too valuable to spend keeping quiet will eventually have no time for God and his brother, but only for himself and for his own follies. . . .

There is a kind of listening with half an ear that presumes already to know what the other person has to say. It is an impatient, inattentive listening, that despises the brother . . . , and it is certain that here, too, our attitude toward our brother only reflects our relationship to God. It is little wonder that we are no longer capable of the greatest service of listening that God has committed to us, that of hearing our brother's confession, if we refuse to give ear to our brother on lesser subjects. . . .

Christians have forgotten that the ministry of listening has been committed to them by Him who is Himself the greatest listener and whose work they should share.[17]

Friendliness

The Christian ambassador expresses his or her love not only in terms of listening, but also in friendliness. Friendships are important, especially to children. Should they be less important to adults? Even between relatives, friendship can be pleasurable. For example, recently I found on my shelves a dusty little book inscribed by my sister. It contains the children's poem "A Friend Is Someone Who Likes You," by Joan Walsh Anglund. This poem speaks of friendship between brother and sister, ushers, or anybody. It also lifts up a problem:

Sometimes you don't know who are your friends.
Sometimes they are there all the time, but you walk right
 past them and don't notice that they like you in a special way.
And then you think you don't have any friends.
Then you must stop hurrying and rushing so fast.[18]

While the Anglund poem conveys a universal message, it has special meaning for the church usher. Friendship is not a problem for children; it is only as we grow older that difficulty arises in the cultivation of friends. In the aging process we tend to be less sure and more suspicious of people, especially newcomers. Then, too, we must learn to contend with our enemies—including those who compete with us in school, in business, and in social relations. Consequently, we become more particular about our friends and more wary of our enemies.

Another problem hampering friendship is the prominent titles ascribed to Jesus. The Bible proudly proclaims Jesus prophet, priest, and king. Jürgen Moltmann observed that each of these titles emerges from an authoritarian society. "The exalted titles express no more than what Christ does—or suffers—for a person. They do not yet describe the fellowship he brings to men and women, new fellowship with God and with their neighbors."[19] But we know Jesus was a friend—particularly to sinners. He used the title friend to describe his relationship with the disciples, and he admonished them to emulate his example of friendship. "Greater love has no man than this, that a man lay down his life for his friends. You are my friends if you do what I command you [John 15:13-14]." Moltmann adds, "In the fellowship of Jesus, the disciples become friends of God. In the fellowship of Jesus, they no longer experience God as Lord, nor only as Father; rather, they experience Him in his inmost nature as Friend."[20] The noted German theologian asks, "What would it be like if Christian congregations and communities were no longer to regard themselves only as 'the community of saints,' or as 'the congregation of the faithful,' but as a 'community of friends'?"[21]

Like other characteristics of an ambassador, friendship is hardly limited to the usher's life; it is the life-style of an entire congregation. However, the usher's prominence and visibility provide him or her with a unique opportunity to express friendship to all who cross the threshold. The individual in the congregation is limited to those in the pew or standing nearby.

The church usher is not an automaton. This person is a warm human being who reaches out in love, inviting others, in effect, to experience God's glad acceptance. True, friendship may be practiced more easily in the church nursery than in the sanctuary, but this part of Jesus' character can be emulated in both places.

> The friendship of Jesus cannot be lived and its friendliness cannot be disseminated when friendship is limited to people who are like ourselves and when it is narrowed down to private life. The messianic feast which Jesus celebrates with his own and with the despised and unregarded is not merely "the marriage of the soul with God"; it is also "the festival of the earth."[22]

Intentional Ministry

"Good morning! Welcome!" is a greeting that makes one want to cross the threshold to attend a church event. These words are not unlike those spoken by an ambassador who welcomes people on behalf of her or his country. The model of ambassador for usher is not only biblical, but also is appropriate to that atmosphere wherein the spirit of love and hospitality predominate. The usher represents God and the whole congregation in helping a person to make the transition from world to church.

Because of the significance of ushering, a church can ill afford to go about the task as one might organize a pick-up team for a softball game.

An Usher's Prayer

O God, you have chosen me not just to be good, but to be good for something. That "something" for me is usher—an ambassador for Christ and his church. Granted the honor of the position, I recognize it is an honor based on service rather than appointment.

As your ambassador, I want to be sensitive to your will and to the needs of people. I want to be an effective dispenser of your love: I want to be hospitable, with openness to all—especially strangers; I want to be a good listener and a friend to everyone.

As your envoy, I want to use the gifts and graces you have given me for your glory and for the good of others. I want to embody Christ in the work I do. In Jesus' name. Amen.

3
CALLED TO BE WELCOMERS

When Jesus said, "I was a stranger and you welcomed me [Matt. 25:35c]," in the parable of the last judgment, he was making what today would be called a psychological observation. People who succeeded in welcoming strangers in this parable were unaware of their effectiveness. The ideal for welcomers may indeed be unconscious graciousness and goodwill, but most of us have to work at it.

We have seen how church ushers have a history and a theology, albeit neglected in the history of the church. Now we look at the psychological aspect of their work. Ushering covers a wide range of experience and includes the needs and motives of people, their thought processes and their feelings and emotions. Psychological principles are followed by persons in various fields: teachers use psychology to help students learn; psychologists write books to help parents rear children; media specialists employ psychology to advertise and sell products; and some people take psychological tests to help them choose their careers. Ushers may be added to this list of people who use psychology.

Even though psychology, as a science, is only slightly more than a hundred years old, its findings relate to ushering at several key points. Environment, body language, and closeness are areas of psychological study that merit the usher's consideration.

Welcomers with an Attractive Environment

Books on nonverbal communication, written primarily by psychologists, usually devote whole sections to the effects of environment on people. Institutions such as banks, hospitals, and schools are quite conscious of their visual effects on customers, patients, and students. Architects and building committees share a similar interest, especially with the church steeple and chancel design. Environmental aspects of parking, walkways, landscape, steps, doorways, and narthex areas seem to get less attention from the planners.

Narthex

Generally, churches are oblivious to the rites of passage and therefore give little or no attention to physical and aesthetic arrangements for entranceways. A notable exception is a church building in which I recently assisted with a funeral. The main entrance in the front of the building, as well as a side entrance, led into a spacious narthex; between the two entrances was a small but attractive parlor. Unfortunately, the color scheme in the narthex was sterile to the eye; two dusty artificial plants at the main entrance detracted from the overall appearance; a scarred piece of furniture placed in the middle of the floor contained Bibles. The simple addition of carpeting, a change in colors, and a few attractive furnishings would have made it an ideal and warm entrance.[1]

Most ushers must accept cramped, unattractive work areas, and live with small space, but dirty floors and/or carpeting, unused bulletins, and strewn literature destroy the morale of ushers. A cleaning job or a fresh coat of paint works wonders to transform a drab, unattractive threshold into inviting space for ushers to demonstate their warmth.

Doors

Another interior arrangement begs consideration by most churches—large imposing doors, usually made of solid wood. Why be so protective in appearance? Unless the doors have glass panes in them or windows beside them, the installation of peepholes can be helpful, especially during inclement weather. An open door is more inviting than a closed one. Then, too, a door that is opened for someone carries with it the unspoken message, "We care about you!"

Yards

What about exterior "supports" for the usher?

Location and architecture help or hinder the usher's work. If people approach a church building that has unkept yards, crumpled sidewalks, unpruned shrubbery, litter, and neither railings nor ramps at steps, the message they receive is, "This church is not caring enough for people, especially the disabled." As with the church interior, the trustees or the property committee can aid the usher by improving the exterior appearance of the building. First impressions are hard to change; this is why they are important. In fact, we have only one chance to make a good first impression!

Human factors detract from or enhance environmental factors. For instance, a church building can be visually pleasing, comfortably arranged, and ideally suited for worship and for interaction of people; but if the welcomers are missing or untrained in performing their task, the value of a church experience is diminished. However, poor facilities can be offset to a great extent by caring ushers who are trained in the art of using verbal and nonverbal symbols. One can serve as a reinforcement for the other.

Welcomers with Effective Body Language

Body language—dubbed kinesics by anthropologist Ray L. Birdwhistell—is not new to the American scene.[2] People have been communicating with nonverbal signs since the first interchange between Adam and Eve. What is new is a spate of research and published articles on the subject. A recent sampling of magazine articles includes the following titles: "Nonverbal Communication: How We Send Emotional Messages,"[3] "How Well Do You Read Body Language?,"[4] "What Your Body Language Says About You,"[5] "Watching Your Every Move: What You Reveal About Yourself Without Saying a Word,"[6] and "Body Talk and Tone of Voice: The Language Without Words."[7]

Phony Body Language

Nonverbal communication specialists are quick to point out the interrelationship between verbal (words) and nonverbal (neither written nor spoken) forms of communication. Nonverbal symbols are usually combined with verbal symbols to reinforce a meaning. What the usher does usually counts more than what the usher says. Unfortunately, a welcomer may verbalize one thing and, unknowingly, cancel these words with contrary body language.

I witnessed an example of the disparity between an usher's words and actions while visiting a church in Columbus, Ohio. An usher courteously welcomed my family and me at the door, but at the conclusion of the service this same usher, along with a fellow usher, passed us standing alone in the sanctuary without even nodding in our direction. They were on their way to the coffee hour in the nearby parlor. Maybe the biblical characters in the good Samaritan story (Luke 10:25-37) were on their way to a coffee hour! What I do know is that nonverbal signs serve to regulate the flow of communication. Their purpose is to encourage visitors, not alienate them, but this is what neglectful symbols may unwittingly do. Nonverbal signs are employed mainly to communicate feeling and, according to most authorities, have a greater impact on people than words.[8]

Greetings

An interesting example of the interplay between the verbal and nonverbal occurs in the process of greeting. Ervin Goffman uses the phrase supportive interchange, to describe this act in his book *Relations in Public*.[9] Greeting behavior does vary between individuals, depending on the circumstance and degree of acquaintance. If the usher and the people being served are acquainted, some show of pleasure is natural.

Another factor needs to be considered in ushering—greeting special people like the elderly and the handicapped. Some individuals require more attention than others. The usher needs to care for everyone, particularly those with special needs.

As stated earlier, treatment of the stranger is a matter of Christian concern. Goffman, who has done extensive research in the field of human interaction, believes that when greetings are performed between strangers, a nod may be sufficient; as the relationship grows, a verbal exchange may follow. The purpose of the initial moves and/or comments in greeting is to open channels of communication.[10] The usher's immediate goal is to convey pleasantness and acceptance, which leads to openness; usually, the opportunity for verbal exchange follows.

Remembering Names

Should one try to know people by name? What place do introductions have in the work of a church usher? "A name," someone has said, "is the sweetest sound in the English langauge." Using a name to welcome a person is always complimentary to the usher and to the guest. Of course, name usage and introductions depend somewhat on the flow of traffic—and on the ability of the usher to remember names. Most ushers can master the art by careful listening and name association. Harry Lorayne and Jerry Lucas tell us the secret of remembering names and faces in their best-selling *The Memory Book*. Use a system "wherein the face tells . . . the name."[11]

The typical usher confesses, "I can remember faces all right, but I can't remember names." Not so, according to Lorayne and Lucas. The first problem is name. Easiest to remember are names like Fox, Paige, Paynter, and Gold—names that create pictures in the mind. Names like Hudson, Jordan, and Shannon have a familiar association. The trouble comes with names that have no English meaning—like Bentavagnia, Antesiewicz, and Smolenski.

Lorayne and Lucas insist that people do not really forget names. They just do not hear them in the first place. Why be embarrassed to say, "I'm sorry I didn't hear your name"? A person's name is one of his or her most prized possessions; he or she is flattered when others want to know it. Asking the person to repeat it is a sign of interest. The Lorayne-Lucas system entails three steps:

1. Take care of the name through association or word substitute. For instance, Bentavagnia (pronounced bent-a-vane-ya) can be pictured as a bent vane.
2. Take care of the face by looking at the person and finding some outstanding feature—say, bushy eyebrows.
3. Associate the substitute word (bent vane for Bentavagnia, for example) with the outstanding facial feature (bushy eyebrows), and in effect you have written this person's name on his or her face, i.e., bushy eyebrows from a bent vane! Thus, you lock the name and face together.

The Memory Book spells out the system simply, convincingly, and in greater detail than I am able to sketch it here.[12] This subject alone could provide a profitable usher training session. According to Goffman, introductions tend to strengthen one's greeting. "When two individuals are introduced by a third, a little dance is likely to occur; faces light up, smiles are exchanged, eyes are addressed, handshakes or hat-doffing may occur, and also inquiries about the other's health—in fact, just the small behaviors we might expect during a greeting."[13]

Smiling

In addition to greeting, usher instructions invariably counsel, "Smile!" Surprisingly, nonverbal communications experts have reservations about the smile; they agree that although the smile is universal, its meaning differs from one culture to another and even within sections of a particular culture. Birdwhistell, who has extensively studied gestures, has concluded, "There is no single facial expression, stance, or body position which conveys the same meaning in all societies."[14] In the United States there are what Birdwhistell calls high-smile areas (such as the South), where people do a lot of smiling, and low-smile areas (such as western New York State), where they do not. His smile research lead him to observe that

> while it was perfectly appropriate (as measured by social response) for a young female to smile among strangers on Peachtree Street in Atlanta, Georgia, such behavior would be highly inappropriate on Main Street in Buffalo, New York. In one

part of the country, an unsmiling individual might be queried as to whether he was "angry about something," while in another, the smiling individual might be asked, "What's funny?"[15]

Other findings by nonverbal specialists also relate to ushering. In general, the experts put a high premium on vocal and facial characteristics. Albert Mehrabian believes that as much as 93 percent of the impact a particular message has depends on nonverbal cues. Receivers value what they hear—and who is saying it—on the basis of nonverbal cues: hair length, voice volume, eye signals, and posture.[16]

Posture

An usher would do well to note these two points concerning posture. The first has to do with body angle: When one is looking over one's shoulder or facing someone at an angle, one is not as caring in effect as if one were facing the person head-on. Leaning is another body message; it communicates more warmth than standing erect.

Graciousness (meaning kindness, pleasantness, and warmth) is an important characteristic for the usher to display. It is a gift and an art, implemented in no small measure by a caring posture. Holding a door open, turning toward the ushered, nodding, or bending—such actions speak louder than words. A conscious use of these will improve the quality of an usher's work.

Interpreting Body Language

Besides having to learn to employ nonverbal symbols, the usher needs to study and interpret the body language of the people served. By observing, the usher can pick up cues that suggest appropriate responses. Concerns of the ushered are usually revealed by their body language; consequently, the trained observer is able to determine whether or not people are strangers by noting their behavior.

Pastor

A key to the experience of welcome lies with the pastor. The pastor and the ushers reflect the tone for the congregation. A church tends to model itself after its leaders. Hospitality in a church may be compared with an orchestra: The pastor is the appointed conductor (the purpose of ordination); the ushers occupy the "first chairs" in different sections; and the members of the congregation occupy the rest of the space. The ideal performance—if one may use this term in its best sense—is the creation of warm, accepting, and supportive vibrations for each person present; each member, then, feels inspired to reach out and touch others. The psychological and theological aspects of this experience are not mutually exclusive.

Faces

Given the historical perspective and theological basis for ushering, one is able to utilize the insights of psychological research to great advantage. Facial communication is but one example. This aspect of body language reminds me of a poem a kindergarten teacher in Greenville, South Carolina, shared with me.

> You don't have to tell
>   how you live each day;
> You don't have to say
>   if you work or you play.
> A tried true barometer
>   serves in its place;
> However you live,
>   it shows in your face.
>
> The false, the deceit,
>   that you bear in your heart
> Will not stay inside
>   where it first got its start,
> For sinew and blood
>   are a thin veil of lace
> What you wear in your heart,
>   you wear in your face.
>
> If your life is unselfish,
>   if for others you live;
> For not what you get,
>   but how much you can give;
> If you live close to God,
>   in His infinite grace,
> You don't have to tell it,
>   it shows in your face.
>   —Author unknown

One's face really "speaks" in ushering. Those whom we serve are directly affected by the spirit behind our words, our facial expressions, and our gestures. Each body movement communicates. The vibes or the emotional impact will be present or absent, depending on our cultivation of the Christian spirit. Indeed, as Peter Scholtes reminds us, passersby will know we are Christians through the love we show.[17] Knowledge, prayer, skill—all are involved in the ministry of ushering.

Welcomers with Proper Closeness

The closeness between usher and ushered is an important factor in nonverbal communications. In the literature of psychology the word distance is used; but when this subject is related to church ushers, "closeness" is more fitting. This area of psychology is called proxemics and has been studied by anthropologist Edward T. Hall. "Hall's 'silent language' of nonverbal communications consists of such culturally determined interactions as the physical distance or closeness maintained between individuals."[18] Society has prescribed what it considers an appropriate distance for interaction between people. In our Western culture, for example, as long as one honors another's space and proper distance, communication moves freely and comfortably. But if personal distance norms are violated, people become nervous, uncomfortable, defensive, and unwilling to communicate. Space "talks!" "In our culture, when we talk to another person, we stand about an arm's length apart. If we see two individuals standing closer, [we] are likely to conclude that either they are lovers or they are plotting a conspiracy."[19] Ronald Applbaum suggests that

> the next time you are chatting with someone, slowly move in. You'll find they will quite unconsciously withdraw to maintain the right distance. In some cultures, the accepted interpersonal distance is smaller. When people from different countries interact, you will find misunderstandings arise because they cannot find a distance that is mutually comfortable. As someone advances on you, you may feel, "He's pushy and overbearing," or "He's falling all over me." On the other hand, if someone withdraws, you may feel, "He's avoiding me; he's trying to hide something," or "He doesn't like me."[20]

Closeness between usher and people, therefore, makes for discomfort or for pleasure, depending on the usher's awareness and skill. Knowledge of the proper distance contributes or detracts from the task, whether the usher is aware of it or not. The absence of an usher or an usher's insensitivity to distance communicates a negative feeling. Wise is the usher who understands and implements a proper closeness in helping people.

Greeters

While the usher's historic function centers at the threshold, the factor of distance for people attending a church event may require additional personnel for the role of welcomer. In some churches the term greeters is used. These persons are often husband-and-wife teams and are usually positioned in heavy traffic areas. Specifically, they are there to complement the usher's work and try to cultivate an atmosphere of friendliness. Greeters may actually be stationed at the doors—introducing visitors to ushers, who then escort them to a pew.

By not having to attend to usher duties, greeters are better able to express welcome than the ushers. Nevertheless, both ushers and greeters are dispensers of hospitality. Sometimes their functions are separate and distinct; at other times the difference in the work is practically indistinguishable. Indeed, an usher may be a greeter one Sunday and an usher the next.

Parking Lots

If the entranceway to the church is separated from the parking areas by walkways, greeters and/or ushers may be located beyond the building. In some large churches parking attendants constitute the first wave of hospitality. An excellent illustration of this is the hospitality program at Garden Grove Community Church, in California, where approximately 7,000 people attend multiple services on a typical Sunday. Eight component groups comprising approximately 350 trained people assist visitors and members in attending the services at Garden Grove. This program is directed by a staff clergyman, who carries the title Minister of Hospitality.

Most churches in urban settings do not have church-owned parking lots. People either walk or travel by bus, taxi, and/or subway to attend services. Here distance is more compact. Even so, no less attention should be given this subject. The absence of ushers and/or greeters automatically conveys an uncaring image; conversely, their presence and appropriate closeness communicate positive vibrations.

Instinctive Affection

The church has often viewed the findings of science with suspicion and distrust. It is, therefore, reassuring when a scientist comes along with an explicit interest in moral and ethical issues; such a person is Iranäus Eibl-Eibesfeldt, a Swiss anthropologist.

Of interest to ushers is the fact that Dr. Eibl-Eibesfeldt believes in an instinctive affectionate bonding drive in all people. In other words, those who are ushered either consciously or unconsciously seek sociability or incorporation into groups. Furthermore, the urge exists for us to form bonds with strangers as well as with friends.[21] If this is true—and I believe it is—then the people whom we serve have a desire for community; they want to be part of a group—apart from any religious considerations. It follows, then, that those who approach the threshold of a religious meeting do so out of interest and sympathy. The usher's task is not to impose a "welcome" on them, but simply to recognize and acknowledge the sense of welcome that is innately theirs.

An Usher's Prayer

God, you have called me to a ministry where love and goodwill are expressed in several ways. I acknowledge my limitations and those of my church. I am a representative of my congregation and part of its physical environment. Help me to make the best of our facilities, regardless of any handicaps we may have.

I realize that my body "talks." Both my words and my actions are important to the people I serve. My nonverbal symbols really "speak!" Grant that they may be supportive, affirming, and effective. May my smile, body angle, and posture all indicate a caring attitude.

Enable me to maintain a proper closeness—a stance that is neither perfunctory nor plastic. Make me knowledgeable and alert to my calling of welcomer. Amen.

4
CALLED TO BE HELPERS

In the preceding chapters church ushers were viewed as doorkeepers, ambassadors, and welcomers—terms that describe their history, theology, and psychology; this final chapter deals with the more practical aspects of their work. An excerpt from 1 Corinthians 12:27-28 supports the usher's role as "helper": "Now you are the body of Christ and individually members of it. And God has appointed in the church first apostles, second prophets, third teachers, then workers of miracles, then healers, *helpers,* administrators, speakers in various kinds of tongues." Note the subject of the text: "*God* has appointed . . . helpers." We have discussed how critical the usher's work at the threshold is to the rites of passage. The Corinthian statement makes explicit what has been implicit all along, that God calls some to help in the church as ushers. If these persons are to fulfill this mission, they must be organized, trained, and efficient. This chapter elaborates the functional side of the usher's work.

Helpers Who Are Organized

Encouragement for some type of organized effort at ushering is found in 1 Corinthians 14:40: "All things should be done decently and *in order.*" The church is first and foremost an "organism"—a body of believers in Jesus Christ, committed to him and the cause of the kingdom. Having said this, however, organization—the bringing together of different elements and functions and people into harmonious and united action—is a means of fullfilling God's purpose. Goals, priorities, and planning are all part of the organized effort to achieve God's mission.

At least four different organization models exist that relate to ushers. Natural, Lackadaisical, Authoritarian, and Participatory. Other models may also be found, but these four are followed in most churches.

Natural Model of Organization

The Natural Model is found in churches where the work is informally arranged. Ushers are instant and spontaneous. Usually they are among the first to arrive at church, greeting those who come after. At offering time one eyes another, and they automatically rise to receive the plates. If more than two ushers are needed, additional nods net the desired number.

This informal organization is found in churches of different sizes. Its success depends on the gifts and graces of the people who lead it. These persons evolve in their roles and migrate to positions of leadership. Surprisingly, they do the job well—without guidelines or job descriptions. A good example is The Church of the Saviour, in Washington, DC. I asked the pastor, the Rev. Gordon Cosby, about the work of his ushers. Dr. Cosby replied, "We do no training and have no instructional materials in the area of ushering. . . . We do have people who sense a real call to this ministry of hospitality. It surely is an important ministry."[1]

The Natural Model seems to work well in churches where people have a sense of call to this ministry. May their tribe increase! One limitation to the model, however, is its tendency toward not cultivating new persons to assume the role of usher; consequently, when death or disability strikes, the whole system suffers and may require months or even years to regain its pattern of efficiency. Blessed is the church that takes a long view in its leader development.

Lackadaisical Model of Organization

If one is to organize or improve the ushering program in a local church, two models should be avoided: the Lackadaisical and the Authoritarian. The Lackadaisical Model is organized along the lines of a week-by-week pickup system: ushers are nabbed at arrival time; bulletins are thrust into their hands; people are seated thoughtlessly and carelessly; and the collection of the offering is performed in a disconnected fashion.

Ushers bring widely divergent assumptions to their job, as concluded from an usher survey conducted in four churches representing various denominational, socioeconomic, cultural, and ethnic stripes. This survey also revealed a variety of views among the ushers of the individual churches. To assume, therefore, that the invitation to this work automatically produces unity of purpose and efficiency in performance is unrealistic.

Authoritarian Model of Organization

Serious defects may also be found at the end of the spectrum opposite the Lackadaisical Model. Unfortunately, the Authoritarian approach to organization is currently in wide use, especially among the more conservative congregations. The system works from the top down rather than from the bottom up, with ushers functioning blindly, often carrying out policy and procedures decided by "somebody else." As one manual puts it, "Ultimate authority for the supervision of the church ushers rests in the hands of the pastor, but usually he is glad to delegate this responsibility on a week-to-week basis to one of the official boards of the church."[2] While this model tends to produce a degree of efficiency in operation, it also produces apathy and indifference on the part of ushers. Unless rules and procedures reflect the feelings and beliefs of those who implement them, the organization tends to be mechanical and lacks motivation. In an extensive treatment of this subject Robert C. Worley writes, "Most rules and procedures were not designed to mobilize or activate members of a congregation. They were designed to maintain control by an elite minority."[3]

Rules and procedures are human inventions, designed to facilitate the work of an usher; they should be open to periodic review and change. Suggestions for usher improvement should be sought from different sources, including the ushers and congregation. If rules are to be faithfully followed in a voluntary organization, the people using them should be involved in making them.

Participatory Model of Organization

The Participatory Model is another viable approach to organizing ushers in the local church. It consists of study by interested persons and recommendations to the governing board, with broad input from pastor, staff, ushers, and congregation. The more people involved, the better the chance of approval and implementation.

A layperson usually leads the usher organization in the local church. In some places this individual is called head usher; in other places, usher coordinator or usher board chairman. The extent of organization depends on the size and needs of a particular congregation. Some people are called to be helpers in this work—but not all. The foremost requirement is commitment to the church; the program is weakened when persons with little or no commitment are asked to serve.

Leaders in an organization tend to emerge in the process of shared or participatory leadership. A key ingredient for success in any voluntary organization is the incorporation of suggestions and recommendations from the volunteers. Some differences of opinion are inevitable and can usually be resolved through discussion and negotiation. Better to have some disagreement in participation than to have agreement in nonparticipation.

Special Services: Weddings

After deciding on the organizational model to be used, ushers in the local church can plan their work and work their plan. Ushers are to be organized for regular services and for special services. While the same persons may be used for both types of services, they usually are not. At a wedding, for example, the ushers may be strangers to the local congregation, coming from different places and with different backgrounds. Since outsiders are unfamiliar with local facilities and procedures, someone—either a regular usher or the pastor—needs to acquaint them with their surroundings and provide instruction if they are to be helpful. Pity the poor usher who knows only how to walk down the aisle and stand at a particular place during the wedding ceremony! A wedding rehearsal is never complete without some usher organization and training. "Conduct yourselves wisely toward outsiders, making the most of the time. Let your speech always be gracious, seasoned with salt, so that you may know how you ought to answer every one [Col. 4:5-6]." How can one possibly carry out this biblical mandate without some knowledge and training.

Special Services: Funerals

The funeral is another occasion for special usher considerations. Although funeral directors are the professional ushers in such a service, their work can be enhanced by assistance from local ushers. Wise is the usher who is aware of and responsive to the special needs of the grieving.

> In addition to listening to what your friend has to say, it is also important to receive his injured and shattered feelings with attitudes that make these feelings seem proper and right. Sometimes a shoulder to cry on is a most important part of the ventilating of deep feelings. To know that someone is willing to feel with you even when you cannot express your feelings very well is important.[4]

At the funeral of a neighboring colleague I was struck by the compassionate attention shown to the bereaved family by the ushers. The body language of one usher in particular was impressive. Her sense of care was obvious by her facial expressions and her closeness to the family. This usher's sympathy and love will be remembered after the words of the officiating clergy have been forgotten. The funeral usher has a unique opportunity to minister in Christ's name.

Nonworship Events

Meetings held at a church are usually public; they include the Sunday service(s), baptisms, weddings, funerals, and church/training events. How can the church be hospitable to visitors if no one is there to meet and greet them? Those planning to attend usually find their way to the meeting place, but how much more pleasurable the experience if representatives are on hand to assist them. Besides, if no representatives are present, visitors may have difficulty locating rest rooms, telephones, and emergency equipment. The absence of an usher or representative to a church-sponsored event carries with it the message, "Take care of yourself!" or "Do the best you can!" I have difficulty squaring this attitude with the biblical commands, "Be hospitable . . . be loving . . . be helpful."

Not long ago, I walked into a church building to see the pastor. Unfortunately, no people or directional signs were around to lead me to his office; so I pursued the trial-and-error method to locate him. I first tried the main building—upstairs and downstairs—but no pastor! Then I entered another building and worked my way through a maze of kindergarten classrooms. After reaching the end of one long hallway I found that another hallway intersected it. I was tempted to toss a coin to help me decide whether to go right or left, but since the intersecting hallway was not long, I chose to turn left. After finding only two more classrooms, I turned back and finally found the pastor's study on the left side of the hallway—one room shy of the last one in the building!

This example of finding one's way through an unfamiliar building represents the feelings a stranger encounters. Directional signs and/or guides are important.

Helpers Who Are Trained

A job that is worth doing is a job worth doing well. If God calls us to a task, then dare we treat it carelessly or lightly? Christian stewardship requires us to use God's gifts in the best way possible. If ushers are to be responsible stewards, they must learn to use their talents to the glory of God. No one is born with knowledge and skills for the job; they are acquired.

Which training model(s) should be used?

Garden Grove Training Program

After deciding on a basic organizational structure, proceed to train the troops. Not many churches are as large as or possess resources like

Garden Grove Community Church, in Garden Grove, California. As Minister of Hospitality, Howard E. Kelley directed the organization and training of 350 people in eight different groups that comprise the hospitality ministry: hospitality center greeters, traffic and parking personnel, hosts and hostesses, tour guides, tower aides, greeters, guest book receptionists, and ushers. In a letter, Kelley stated that the

> ushers are carefully and individually selected through a process that involves a private interview. . . . They are required to attend a seven-week training course that fully acquaints them with [the] church, related ministries and the techniques and niceties of ushering.
> Once they begin to serve, they are required to attend briefing sessions each Sunday morning prior to the service in which they serve. The purpose of this session is to give them their assignments for the day and to provide them with pertinent information about the day's activities.[5]

Admittedly, the Garden Grove training plan is unique. But any church accustomed to approximately 7,000 people attending multiple services on a typical Sunday would have to conduct a hospitality program that was this elaborate!

Experiential Learning

One approach to learning is the experiential method, advocated by Robert Arthur Dow.[6] The usher learns through encounter, by doing. To be effective, experiential education must be (1) current in its information; (2) eclectic in its findings; (3) not wedded to particular structure, forms, and dogmas; and (4) dynamic.

> Many disciplines are struggling against obsolescence. New trends force us to consider new ways of coping with each new crisis. To refashion the old, to retrieve the valued, and to grasp the vital among the innovative is the business of experiential education. We must weigh both old and new through a selective process, create a meaningful synthesis that is relative to the here and now, in the full knowledge that this movement, too, will pass.[7]

Usher groups in local churches would do well to combine theoretical training with hands-on experience. What is successful in one church may not work in another. Ushering must be experienced if it is to be learned. Decisions to be made by a local church include length of training, resources for training, recruitment for training, and evaluations of training.

I recommend at least four one-hour sessions—one for each section of this book. Conceivably, the training sessions could be held on four consecutive nights, but four consecutive weeks or months is better. Although it is possible to combine this instruction with other leadership concerns, I do not advise it. A subject as important and as far-reaching as ushering merits individual attention. In some churches this training may have to be scheduled as part of a larger meeting, but this should be a last resort.

What are the usher-training resources?

Resources

A manual such as this one might well provide the text for a training course. In addition, most churches have members with professions that relate to the usher's work, i.e., teachers, administrators, personnel directors, psychologists, counselors, and so on. Furthermore, the local library probably has resources that can be made available to interested individuals and/or groups. Professors in nearby colleges, universities, or seminaries can also contribute to the cause. While resources are not limitless, especially in the line of printed and visual materials, they are adequate for the enterprising leader.

Recruitment

Everybody's business is nobody's business, so some plan for recruitment must be selected. One that I recommend consists of six steps:

1. Conduct an usher survey.
2. Send a letter to selected respondents.
3. Print notices in the bulletin.
4. Do personal cultivation.
5. Mail card reminders.
6. Telephone a personal reminder.

Usher Survey

The usher survey, to be conducted two to three months before the training program begins, has at least two important benefits: It lets the congregation know that their views about the usher's work are important in helping to design a training program, and it sets up a method for evaluating the training results. People are more responsible if their opinions are sought. The survey should contain the following choices, placed to the right of the questions:

Strongly agree	Agree	Uncertain	Disagree	Strongly disagree
☐	☐	☐	☐	☐

—with the request that *one* of the above be checked. The "before" survey can be numbered 1, 2, 3, 4, and 5, which, combined and averaged, will yield an opinion profile for the church. An "after" training survey using the same questions but on a different color paper will indicate the areas of changed opinion.

The following questions, by no means exhaustive, may be included in such a survey. They relate to the contents of this manual.

I. Ushering consists of:
    Greeting people before the service
    Greeting people after the service
    Distributing bulletins
    Communicating Christian love
    Opening doors
    Seating people
    Receiving the offering
    Getting to know people
    Helping strangers feel at home
    Representing Jesus and his love
    Introducing visitors/strangers
    Accepting all people
    Assisting in emergencies (i.e., illness)
    Noting absence of regular attenders

II. I usher for the following reasons:
    To provide a needed service
    To fulfill a sense of duty
    To fulfill a desire to serve
    To respond to pressure to serve
    To meet people
    To respond to the biblical mandate
    To promote church attendance
    To provide hospitality
    To complement greeters, minister, etc.
    To express the joy of the Christian life

III. Ushers should include:
- Only men
- Only women
- Both men and women
- Men, women, and youth
- Volunteers
- Only selected persons
- Only church members

IV. Ushering should be provided for:
- All worship services
- Special services: weddings, funerals, etc.
- Other church events: dinners, musicals, etc.
- Community groups using the facility

V. Ushering should include:
- Some training and/or instructions
- History/mechanics knowledge of ushering
- A broadened awareness of hospitality
- Checking on heating, cooling, lighting, etc.
- Counting attendance, if necessary

Letter to Selected Respondents

The second step in this recruitment plan consists of a letter sent to respondents who are interested in the training program, signed by the head usher and/or pastor.

(date)

Dear (name):

Thank you for your recent response to the usher survey, which we took in our church in (name of month). Your participation helped our (name of programming body) to decide on a training program that we think will improve this important ministry at (name of church).

These four nights . . . .
at (name of church)
in (name of city)
(time)

> Ushers: An Embodiment of the Gospel in the Local Church
> (Day and date): "Called to Be Doorkeepers"
> (Day and date): "Called to Be Ambassadors"
> (Day and date): "Called to Be Welcomers"
> (Day and date): "Called to Be Helpers"
> . . . may change an usher's life
>
> Please keep this training opportunity in mind. It could mean much to you as well as the people we serve.
>
> Sincerely,

Step two is completed with the mailing of the letter to selected respondents a month before the first scheduled training session is to begin.

Bulletin Notices

Step three involves notices appearing in the bulletin on the four Sundays preceding the training. These notices could relate to the content of the four sessions. (The four notices may be reprinted in local church bulletins.)

Notice #1: USHER TRAINING ANNOUNCED

What is an usher? What is this person supposed to be and to do? What does the Bible have to say about ushering? These and other questions will be explored in a series of usher training events scheduled for our church on (list of dates).

If you are now an usher, or if you think you would like to become one, this is your chance to experience some valuable training—to be led by (name of leader), beginning (date of first session). The (name of programming body) believes this is an important learning opportunity for the people of our church.

Notice #2: USHER TRAINING OPEN TO ALL

A recent usher survey in our church revealed much interest in this subject. Opinions were varied and questions were raised on a host of biblical images and concepts that relate to ushering.

An usher training course, set for our church on (list of dates) proposes to look at this subject through the lenses of Christian love, hospitality, the kingdom of God, and the Body of Christ—important biblical themes!

If you are now an usher, or if you think you would like to become one, please plan to join us at the first session on (date).

Notice #3:   USHER TRAINING NEARS

"I was a stranger and you welcomed me." Jesus said that, you may recall, in the parable of the last judgment (Matthew 25:35c). This comment will be considered for its application to modern ushers in a series of sessions for our church on (list of dates).

How do ushers communicate "welcome" to the people? What can a church do to provide for a pleasant environment? When should a name be remembered—and how?

If you are an usher or would consider becoming one, this training opportunity is what you've been looking for!

Notice #4:   USHER TRAINING BEGINS

The long-heralded usher-training program at (name of church) begins on (day, date, time, and place). If you are now an usher, or think you would like to become one, you are encouraged to attend this excellent training series that has been especially designed for our church.

Ushers are important helpers at (name of church) and require a knowledge of facilities, policies, emergency procedures, and other functions to do their job well.

This usher training views the subject from the standpoint of its historical, theological, psychological, and practical dimensions and is open to all interested persons.

Personal Cultivation

There is no substitute for a personal invitation. The fourth step in this recruitment plan is personal cultivation of attendance by those committed to the program. By excerpting the center section of the letter on pages 51-52 and having it attractively printed on a card, the solicitor can provide the prospective attendant with the essential details. Promoters for the usher training include the pastor and the head usher.

Mailed Reminder

Step five in this recruitment drive is a mailed reminder. One may wish to take advantage of the card already printed and used by the promoters. A color change in paper stock is a more imaginative way of promoting than the use of the same colored card for the entire effort.

Telephone Reminder

The sixth and final step is the telephone reminder. This step should be initiated on the third and second days, respectively, before the training begins. Busy people do not object to being reminded of important events.

The virtue of this plan of usher-training recruitment is that it makes everybody's business *somebody's* business! There are other ways. The timetable and extent of promotion will vary from church to church. Establishing some training as a goal, keeping it as a priority before the people, and having some plan of promotion are necessary for success.

What about training evaluations?

Evaluations

The most important evaluations of any training experience are personal ones—a sense of growth by the participant, complimentary remarks at the drugstore or across the backyard fence. A church's image is nebulous but important; it helps to determine a church's influence and outreach. Attendance is another barometer to watch in the evaluation process. Success breeds success.

I have already indicated that "before" and "after" surveys can be taken. These are measurable results and will help the local church determine the strengths of the project, as well as improvements that may be made in similar ventures in the future.

Adequate training for ushers is essential. Two hundred years ago Alexander Pope—before he was 21—wrote his brilliant *An Essay on Criticism,* in which he said, "A little learning is a dang'rous thing."[8] Beware of the Pope comment when designing plans for usher training! William Allen White added a corrective to the Pope comment: "A little learning is not a dangerous thing to one who does not mistake it for a great deal."[9]

Helpers Who Are Efficient

To speak of the usher's efficiency is to talk about the content or techniques of the work. A helpful usher is one who is

- responsible in the assignment.
- aware of the church's facilities.
- sensitive to safety.
- aware of medical resources.
- knowledgeable about service procedures.
- anxious to help with practical needs.

Because people arrive at a service several minutes before it begins, the usher should report for duty at an agreed time, usually twenty to thirty minutes before the service, when the head usher or captain designates door and aisle assignments. If one cannot serve at the scheduled time, this information should be conveyed in time to secure a replacement.

Facilities

Some churches have a sexton on duty during a service, but this is more the exception than the rule. Usually it is the usher who is responsible for ventilation, lighting, heating/air conditioning, and sound/recording equipment. The trustees or maintenance committee may have this responsibility. The usher's chief concern is the comfort of the people. He or she should know the location of rest rooms, telephones, and church nursery.

Unless the traffic is heavy, the usher may wish to respond, "Let me show you," leading the inquirer toward the needed facility. A few steps express more of a caring attitude than verbal directions. The helpful, efficient usher responds appropriately to all questions.

Safety

Safety is one of the usher's chief concerns. Fire safety is one aspect of this concern.[10] A few years ago in our town, a large congregation had just completed its new sanctuary when the boiler suddenly back-flashed, and the worshipers had to be evacuated during a morning service. Every congregation needs a plan of evacuation in case of emergency.

Are ushers familiar with all exits? Are exits left unlocked during an assembly? Is there easy access by aisles to each exit? What about fire extinguishers? Are they visible? Do you know their number, location, and rating? One fire extinguisher is usually required for every 75 to 100 feet of walking space, and all extinguishers are to be inspected annually. Generally, fire inspectors do not make routine inspections of churches; therefore, the initiative for fire safety lies with local church officials.

One of my concerns for fire safety comes during the annual Christmas carol and candlelight service. I am always afraid that someone's hair will be singed or that a lighted candle will be accidentally dropped by a young child. Is a fire extinguisher operative and ready for such an event?

Medical Emergency

Medical emergencies sometimes occur during a service; someone may faint or suddenly become ill. The usher should be aware of the location of a doctor or a nurse who may be in attendance, in case their services are needed. Also, the usher should know the location of emergency equipment, such as a wheelchair, a stretcher, blankets, an oxygen tank, and first aid supplies.

Rarely, a person who is mentally ill interrupts a service. Such a person should be met calmly by two ushers who escort the person quietly and firmly from the service to a place where further aid or care may be provided. The usher requests but does not tell a worshiper what to do; nor does the usher argue or become irritated. To be efficient, the usher must be both knowledgeable and disciplined.

Seating Procedures

The main entranceway tends to become crowded just before a service begins.

> If experience shows that many people coming in the front door wish to talk to the usher stationed there, then two or more ushers should be available at the door. When the usher who gives the greeting becomes engaged in conversation, he will step away from the door and finish the conversation out of the way. The second usher, in the meanwhile, steps forward and takes the place of the first, and carries on.[11]

Unless the worshiper makes a request or the seating habit is known, the usher may ask, "What about halfway down on the right?" or "I have two seats on the aisle" or "I believe you will enjoy the service if you are seated. . . ." When the question "Where would you like to be seated?" is asked, the usher automatically limits the seating possibilities. Many persons appreciate the usher's offer of help in choosing a seat. "If the usher walks too fast, people will lag behind and feel very much alone. They even may slip into a seat near the back and leave the usher standing with no one to seat."[12] By not handing out the bulletin until a worshiper has reached his or her seat, the usher lessens the risk of going one way and the worshiper another! "An usher never points to a seat and sends people off down the aisle by themselves. He shows them to their seats personally."[13]

What about those who are accustomed to a favorite pew and who head for it, spurning the usher's offer of assistance? Their wishes, of course, are to be respected. However, the experienced usher will anticipate their habits, and will be one step ahead of them, offering them a bulletin at their accustomed spot.

In this world we shall have tribulation and some people who will not move over! What about them? Kindness, patience, tolerance—these help, as well as a general church emphasis on Christian hospitality. The usher can take courage from the fact that he or she is a servant, never a magician. Jesus loved people as they were—even those, I suspect, who would not budge in the pew! An usher must do likewise.

The efficient usher is familiar with church procedures in seating latecomers. Many churches indicate times for this by using asterisks in the order of worship. Since visitors may not know the worship hour, at least one usher should remain at or near the entranceway, to seat those who arrive after the service has begun. Latecomers should be seated as quickly and as inconspicuously as possible. A rule of thumb is not to interrupt special music, prayers, creeds, or the reading of scripture. An usher's request to wait until a convenient time to enter is usually respected.

The efficient usher keeps abreast of available seats. As much as possible, persons are seated from the front to the rear. The usher *leads* the worshiper—never follows. The simple matter of furnishing a bulletin at the seat so that it can be read right side up is a sign of thoughtfulness. In large gatherings people do not mind an usher leaning over courteously and whispering, "Would you please move down the pew a little?" Leslie Parrott emphasizes kindness in the usher's conversation—never negative statements or judgmental remarks.[14] Some examples are:

> *Negative:* "You cannot go in now."
> *Positive:* "I will seat you in just a moment."
>
> *Negative:* "You're late! You'll have to sit in the back."
> *Positive:* "Since the service has started, I'll try to find a seat for you near the back."
>
> *Negative:* "At your age, I suppose you need a hearing aid."
> *Positive:* "There are some good seats up front where everyone can see and hear the best."

People attend a church service to be lifted up not to be put down.

Offering

Ushers can easily take the offering in such a way as to add to the beauty of the service. By stepping together, by making left or right turns on the basis of prior agreement, by carrying the plates at waist level, and by proceeding orderly to receive the offering, the act of dedication can be a high point in the service. In receiving the offering, ushers on the inside center aisle take the odd-numbered pews; outside ushers, the even-numbered. This avoids hesitation or the passing of the plate down the same pew twice. In taking the offering, ushers face the rear as much as possible; they also try to stay together, pausing briefly, if necessary.

Communion

Communion practices differ from denomination to denomination. In churches that invite worshipers to come forward for communion, ushers need to give clear directions, inviting no more to the kneeling rail than can be comfortably accommodated. Whether ushers themselves commune first or last depends on local custom. Again, orderly movement is important to the worship atmosphere.

A Checklist of Duties

In some churches ushers do more than greet and seat people, and receive the offering. The following list of usher responsibilities was compiled from a recent survey of churches throughout the country.

1. Secure additional chairs for overflow crowd; return center-aisle chairs after the first stanza of the final hymn.
2. Post hymn selections on hymn boards.
3. Compile/collect attendance reports.
4. Replace hymnals and Bibles in the racks after the service.
5. Place kneelers in an upright position after the service.
6. Remove all loose papers/bulletins to nearby receptacle.
7. Readjust the thermostats after the service.
8. Place plastic bags over the Christian/American flags.
9. Take lost articles to the church office.
10. Turn off the lights.
11. Close and lock the doors.
12. Turn off the speaker system.
13. Escort parents/sponsors for baptismal services.
14. Replenish pew envelopes and visitor registration cards/pads.
15. Secure reserved pews, using pew reservation ropes, for special occasions, such as Scout Sunday, fraternal groups, classes, and so on.
16. Obtain the names of visitors (especially those from out of town) to give to the minister so they can be welcomed publicly.

One can master the techniques and niceties of ushering with a minimum amount of training and experience. More difficult is elevating the work from the level of the routine and mechanical. Regardless of traditions and patterns, the usher can become an embodiment of the gospel in the local church.

In a recent publication Walter Wink concluded with comments that have important relevance for the church usher.[15] To paraphrase Wink's comments, the work to be done asks that you struggle to give up the old self to become a different kind of usher—an artist of doing, an artist of action, an artist who can use one's physical self. The usher's work calls for heart and muscle and feeling that have emotions in them. In ushering, you reach out and become a partner with Someone Else. In this encounter, power enters that makes for fresh insight into yourself as well as the people you serve. It is when you become willing to change and grow and have an experience richer than you are able to have on your own that you become your best self. The usher who is doorkeeper, ambassador, welcomer, and helper stands a good chance of becoming this kind of person.

An Usher's Prayer

O God, you have called me to be a helper in your church. I recognize that some order is needed if I am to be effective. As your steward, I need to make the best use of your gifts in ushering. To be a disciple is to be a learner; help me to take advantage of the learning opportunities that are mine.

I want to be a responsible usher. I want to be a knowledgeable usher. I want to be sensitive to safety, and I want to be aware of procedures in our church, so I can be helpful in every way possible.

I am only one usher—but I am *one.* Help me faithfully to fulfill the duties of this work. In Jesus' name. Amen.

NOTES

1: Called to Be Doorkeepers

1. Arnold van Gennep, *The Rites of Passage,* trans. by Monika B. Vizedom and Gabrielle L. Caffee (Chicago: University of Chicago Press, 1960). Van Gennep's original manuscript was published in 1909.
2. Mircea Eliade, *The Sacred and the Profane,* trans. from the French by Willard R. Trask (New York: Harcourt Brace Jovanovich, 1959).
3. Ibid., p. 25.
4. *Theological Dictionary of the Old Testament,* Vol. 1, ed. by G. Johannes Botterweck and Helmer Ringgren (Grand Rapids: William B. Eerdmans, 1975), pp. 107-16.
5. An excellent example showing the affinity between house and temple is a sanctuary at Tepe Gawra in northern Mesopotamia, architecturally so similar to a house that only the presence of an altar allows it to be so distinguished. A drawing may be found in Sigfried Giedion, *The Eternal Present* (New York: Pantheon Books, 1963), p. 190. This drawing is also cited by Lloyd R. Bailey in "Sacred Places," Part II of the series *The Sacred in Ancient Israel and the Near East* (Evanston: Religion and Ethics Institute, Inc., 1981).
6. Eliade, *The Sacred and the Profane,* op. cit. p. 25.
7. J.C. Groce, Jr., *Main Stream,* newsletter of Main Street United Methodist Church, Kernersville, NC, April 30, 1980.
8. Harrell F. Beck, "Neighbor," *The Interpreter's Dictionary of the Bible,* Vol. 3, ed. by Emory Stevens Bucke (Nashville: Abingdon Press, 1962), pp. 534-35.
9. William Morris, ed., *The American Heritage Dictionary of the English Language* (Boston: Houghton Mifflin, 1979).
10. T.M. Mauch, "Sojourner," *The Interpreter's Dictionary of the Bible,* Vol. 4, ed. by Emory Stevens Bucke (Nashville: Abingdon Press, 1962), pp. 397-99.
11. From a conversation with the Rev. Robert A. Lewis, a United Church of Christ minister.
12. D.W. Riddle, "Early Christian Hospitality," *Journal of Biblical Literature,* Vol. 57 (1938), p. 145.
13. Henry Bettenson, ed. *Documents of the Christian Church* (New York: Oxford University Press, 1947), p. 92.
14. Riddle, "Early Christian Hospitality," op. cit., p. 151.
15. Wayne A. Meeks, "Imagining the Early Christians: Some Problems in an Introductory Course in the New Testament," *Perspectives in Religious Studies,* Spring 1975, pp. 3-12.
16. Ibid., p. 10.
17. George H. Williams, "The Ministry of the Ante-Nicene Church," *The Ministry in Historical Perspectives,* ed. by H. Richard Niebuhr and Daniel D. Williams (New York: Harper & Row, 1956), p. 51.
18. Pierre de Puniet, *The Roman Pontifical: A History and Commentary,* trans. by Mildred Vernon Harcourt (New York: Longmans, Green, 1932), p. 128.

The *Statuta Ecclesiae Antiqua,* a canonical collection from South Gaul in the fifth century contains the following prayer for the ordination of a porter: (He is given keys.) "So act as if you were soon to be called to give an account to God for the things which are guarded by these keys."

19. Ibid., p. 129. The *Lexikon fur Theologie und Kirche* (2d ed.), Vol. 7, collection 1286 "Ostiarier" by Theodor Schitzler (1962) says the following: "In the 4th century, the Ostiariate became a transitional stage to the higher orders, without ceasing to be a real office. Gradually, however, he was replaced by the lay mansionarius who were very numerous in the early Middle Ages, Hagia Sophia in Constantinople having several hundred. The title if not the real function was revived in 5th century Gaul but it was still basically a step to the priesthood."
20. Msgr. Carroll E. Satterfield, S.T.D., *Dogmatic Tract on the Sacraments* (Emmitsburg, MD: Mount Saint Mary's Seminary Press, 1976), p. 69.
21. H. Achelis, "Ostiarius," *The New Schaff-Herzog Encyclopaedia of Religious Knowledge,* Vol. 8, ed. by Samuel Macauley Jackson (Grand Rapids: Baker Book House, 1950), p. 283.
22. From a personal letter dated February 2, 1981. Used with permission.
23. Leslie Parrott, *The Usher's Manual* (Grand Rapids: Zondervan, 1970), p. 20.
24. Bernard A. Weisberger, *They Gathered at the River* (Boston: Little, Brown, 1958), p. 207.
25. Timothy Lawrence Smith, *Called Unto Holiness* (Kansas City, MO: Nazarene Publishing House, 1962), p. 120.
26. Mark R. Moore, *The Ministry of Ushering* (Kansas City, MO: Beacon Hill Press, 1957), p. 13.
27. *Principles of Church Ushering* (New York: Church Ushers Association of New York, 1951), p. 1.
28. Washington Gladden, *Church and Parish Problems* (New York: The Thwing Co., 1911).
29. Denise K. Akey, ed., *Encyclopaedia of Associations,* Vol. 1 (15th ed.; Detroit: Gale Research Co., 1980), p. 1082. For information on the national ushers association, write to Isaac N. Nelson, United Church Ushers Association, 3202 Adador Dr., Landover, MD 20785.
30. Willis O. Garrett, *Church Ushers' Manual* (Old Tappan, NJ: Fleming H. Revell, 1924).
31. Gene Flood, "This Way, Please" *Extension,* Vol. 35 (August 1940), pp. 22ff.
32. "Andy Frain, 'Usher King,' Dies," *The New York Times,* March 26, 1964, p. 35.
33. Ibid.
34. Moore, *The Ministry of Ushering,* op. cit., p. 26.
35. Ibid.
36. Homer J.R. Elford, *A Guide to Church Ushering* (Nashville: Abingdon Press, 1961); Alvin D. Johnson, *The Work of the Usher* (Valley Forge, PA: Judson Press, 1966); Parrott, *The Usher's Manual,* op. cit; David R. Enlow, *Church Usher: Servant of God* (Harrisburg, PA: Christian Publications, 1980).

2: Called to Be Ambassadors

1. David R. Enlow, *Church Usher: Servant of God* (Harrisburg, PA: Christian Publications, 1980).

2. O.E. Evans, "Kingdom of God," *The Interpreter's Dictionary of the Bible,* Vol. 3, ed. by Emory Stevens Bucke (Nashville: Abingdon Press, 1962), p. 19.
3. Ibid., p. 23.
4. Paul S. Minear, *Images of the Church in the New Testament* (Philadelphia: Westminster Press, 1960), pp. 268-69.
5. Ibid., p. 194.
6. In George S. Hendry, *The Gospel of the Incarnation* (Philadelphia: Westminster Press, 1958), p. 148.
7. Ibid., pp. 154-55.
8. Robin Scroggs, *Paul for a New Day* (Philadelphia: Fortress Press, 1977), pp. 42-45.
9. Ibid., pp. 44-45.
10. Ibid., pp. 47-48.
11. Ibid.
12. *Pulpit Resource* (Anaheim, CA: Pulpit Resource, Inc. 1979), Vol. 7, No. 2 (Second Quarter, 1979), p. 24.
13. Norman A. Desrosiers, "The Grief of Trying to Join a Church," *Circuit Rider* (Nashville: United Methodist Publishing House), February 1981, p. 13.
14. *Pulpit Resource* (Anaheim, CA: Pulpit Resource, Inc., 1980), Vol. 8, No. 2 (Second Quarter, 1980), pp. 16-17. Used with permission.
15. Henri J.M. Nouwen, *Reaching Out* (Garden City: Doubleday, 1975), p. 46.
16. Ibid., p. 59.
17. Dietrich Bonhoeffer, *Life Together,* trans. and with an introduction by John W. Doberstein (New York: Harper & Row, 1954), pp. 97-99.
18. Joan Walsh Anglund, *A Friend Is Someone Who Likes You* (New York: Harcourt Brace Jovanovich, 1958). Used with permission.
19. Jürgen Moltmann, *The Passion for Life,* trans. with an introduction by M. Douglas Meeks (Philadelphia: Fortress Press, 1978), p. 55. Used with permission.
20. Ibid., p. 57.
21. Ibid. p. 62.
22. Jürgen Moltmann, *The Church in the Power of the Spirit,* trans. from the German by Margaret Kohl (New York: Harper & Row, 1977), p. 121.

3: Called to Be Welcomers

1. Linda R. Heun and Richard E. Heun, *Developing Skills for Human Interaction* (Columbus: Charles E. Merrill Pub. Co., 1975), pp. 42-43. The authors list seven environmental factors: color choice, sounds present, physical comfort, smells, objects present, purpose of room, and potential for interaction allowed by special relations. Such a checklist can guide those who are planning construction, renovation, or the rearrangement of facilities.
2. Ray L. Birdwhistell, *Introduction to Kinesics* (Louisville: University of Louisville Press, 1952).
3. Ernst G. Beier, "Nonverbal Communication: How We Send Emotional Messages," *Psychology Today,* October 1974, pp. 68ff.

4. Dane Archer and Robert M. Akert, "How Well Do You Read Body Language?" *Psychology Today,* October 1977, pp. 68ff.
5. Maxine Lucille Fiel and Mary-Ellen Banaschek, "What Your Body Language Says About You," *Mademoiselle,* December 1978, pp. 154ff.
6. J. Marks, "Watching Your Every Move: What You Reveal About Yourself Without Saying a Word," *Teen,* July 1979, pp. 36ff.
7. Robert Rosenthal et al., "Body Talk and Tone of Voice: The Language Without Words," *Psychology Today,* September 1974, pp. 64-68.
8. Beier, "Nonverbal Communication," op. cit., p. 53.
9. Erving Goffman, *Relations in Public* (New York: Basic Books, 1971), pp. 62-94.
10. Ibid., p. 74.
11. Harry Lorayne and Jerry Lucas, *The Memory Book* (New York: Ballantine Books, 1974), p. 51.
12. Ibid., chapter 8, pp. 50-72.
13. Goffman, *Relations in Public,* op. cit., p. 78.
14. Flora Davis, "The Way We Speak 'Body Language,' " *The New York Times Magazine,* May 31, 1970, pp. 8ff.
15. Ray L. Birdwhistell, *Kinesics and Context* (Philadelphia: University of Pennsylvania Press, 1970), p. 31.
16. Ronald L. Applbaum et al., *Fundamental Concepts in Human Communication* (San Francisco: Canfield Press, 1973), p. 110.
17. See Peter Scholtes, "They'll Know We Are Christians by Our Love," *The Genesis Songbook,* compiled by Carlton R. Young (Carol Stream, IL: Agape, 1973), No. 34; Tertullian, *Apologeticus.*
18. George N. Gordon, "Communication," *The New Encyclopaedia Britannica,* 15th ed. (Chicago: Encyclopaedia Britannica, Inc., 1974), Vol. 4, p. 1008. At the end of the article, a biographical entry calls attention to Edward T. Hall's *The Hidden Dimension* (1966): An unconventional anthropological study of "proxemics" and allied concerns, illustrated by empirical evidence, drawings, and photographs (written with style and humor for the general reader).
19. Applbaum et al., *Fundamental Concepts in Human Communication,* op. cit., p. 111.
20. Ibid.
21. Irenäus Eibl-Eibesfeldt, *Love and Hate: The Natural History of Behavior Patterns,* trans. by Geoffrey Strachan (New York: Holt, Rinehart & Winston, 1971), p. 6.

4: Called to Be Helpers

1. From letter dated November 19, 1980. Used with permission.
2. David R. Enlow, *Church Usher: Servant of God* (Harrisburg, PA: Christian Publications, 1980), p. 27.
3. Robert C. Worley, *A Gathering of Strangers* (Philadelphia: Westminster Press, 1976), p. 51.
4. Edgar N. Jackson, *For the Living* (Des Moines: Meredith Publishing Co., 1963), p. 31.
5. From letter dated November 7, 1980. Used with permission.
6. Robert Arthur Dow, *Learning Through Encounter* (Valley Forge, PA: Judson Press, 1971), pp. 28-37.

7. Ibid., p. 28.
8. Quoted in *The Oxford Book of Quotations* (2d ed.; London: Oxford University Press, 1966).
9. In Laurence J. Peter, *Peter's Quotations* (New York: Bantam Books, 1977), p. 299.
10. *Fire Prevention Code* (New York: American Insurance Association, 1970).
11. *Principles of Church Ushering* (New York: Church Ushers Association of New York, 1951), p. 11.
12. Leslie Parrott, *The Usher's Manual* (Grand Rapids: Zondervan, 1970), p. 33.
13. Ibid.
14. Ibid., p. 31.
15. Walter Wink, "The Preacher as Artist," *The Christian Ministry*, Vol. 12, No. 2 (March 1981), pp. 32-34.